SOLVING

SOUL

STORMS

Become **STORM-PROOF** *rather than* **STORM-FREE!**

by

Using God's remedies for man's problems!

NORMAN R. HEMPHILL

Editorial Services:
Solution Resources, Inc.
Sue Layman-Fincher,
P.O. Box 1295, Albany, TX 76430-1295
915/762-3631

Cover Design by
Dreamz Graphics
6300 Westcreek Dr.
Ft. Worth, TX 76113
817/346-6290

Published by
All Nations Ministries
Dr. Roger Sapp
P.O. Box 92874, Southlake, TX 76092
817/514-0653

Unless otherwise noted, all scripture quotations are from
The Amplified Bible, Copyright ©, 1965,
By Zondervan Publishing House. Used by permission.

Scripture quotations marked NIV are from the Holy Bible,
New International Version. Copyright © 1973,
1978, 1984, International Bible Society. Used by permission.

Scripture quotations marked NASB are from the
New American Standard Bible. Copyright © 1960,
1962, 1963, 1968, 1971, 1972, 1973, 1975, 1977, 1990
by the Lockman Foundation.
Used by permission.

ISBN: 0-9702341-0-4

Printed in the United States by:
Morris Publishing
3212 East Highway 30
Kearney, NE 68847
1-800-650-7888

ACKNOWLEDGEMENTS

The existence of this book is the result of the suggestions by many that believed God had something to say through me and the topics I have been teaching to His children. Maria Cantu and a neighborhood Bible study of sisters and brothers contributed greatly to its genesis by their prayers and assistance. Members of Shady Grove Church in Grand Prairie, TX. who attended my class on Baptisms in our First Principles classes offered words of affirmation and encouragement for this book to be completed.

There have been decades of teachers, pastors and evangelists who spoke through books, in person, on radio, television and tapes sharing revelation from God. The Biblical light contained in those revelations has been an inspiration to me and shines on the pages of this book.

Sue Layman-Fincher spent many hours editing this book. Thanks, Sue, for taking my words and intentions, and setting them in a presentable way. I also appreciate Dr. Roger Sapp, whose advice, help and suggestions I greatly treasure.

I must thank my daughters, Norma Randall and Versia Southerland for their lives of serving the Lord Jesus. Their lives taught me that God's grace could correct even my parenting errors.

Most importantly, I want to thank my life's partner and precious help-meet from God ~ my wife of almost fifty years, and still my best friend, Joyce. The subjects and countless hours of Bible study that contributed to this book's existence came from the in-depth discussions, challenges and questions we have had. Thank you, my darling.

Thanks also to the many whose names are not listed here. It was not an intentional oversight. Please know that God is very aware of your contribution and will subsequently bless you.

May you, the reader, benefit from God's freeing work contained herein.

TABLE OF CONTENTS

Chapter

Introduction   1

1.   Instant Resolution   3

2.   Defining Terms   8

3.   Questioning God   28

4.   Types and Origins of Attacks   37

5.   Root Causes and Associated Attacks   52

6.   God's Repair Kit   74

7.   God's Armor & Weapons   87

8.   Unholy Soul-Ties   102

9.   Breaking Curses   114

10.   Bloodlines and Ancestral/
      Environmental Iniquities   125

11.   Demonization — Roots & Fruit   130

12.   The Necessity of Change   155

TABLE OF CONTENTS

Chapter

13.   Relationships   166

14.   Reaction or Response   185

15.   Walking in Victory   189

       Conclusion   207

INTRODUCTION

I grew up in the northwestern part of Texas where a lot of cotton was grown. In the decades of the 1940's and 1950's (my boyhood days), cotton was harvested in late October and November.

It was the same time the 'blue northers' blew through that region, sometimes-bringing rain and ice.

In those days, the maturing cotton would string four to twelve inches out of the boll, exposing itself to the damaging effects of these 'blue northers.' It left the quality and the price of the cotton diminished.

Agricultural scientists then developed a breed of cotton, which upon maturation, would stay in the boll rather than string out. This resulted in only the fringe of the outside area of the cotton being affected by bad weather. It was labeled "storm-proof" cotton.

After I became a believer in Jesus Christ, God reminded me of this story and said to me, "Most of My children are busy asking Me to *remove* the storms from their lives. Tell them I want their request to be that they become *storm-proof* rather than *storm free*."

Lord, I pray for a life that is
***storm-proof* not necessarily *storm-free*!**
But I want no storm that You do not bring or allow,
In Jesus' Name!

Storms *will* come in this life. Let God help us to become *storm proof* while the storm rages. These storms are ones that attack primarily the *soul* of man. Therefore, I'll call them *soul storms*.

If you and I will prayerfully consider and meditate on how God can use what we are facing and going through to mold us into Jesus' image, it will make the journey of the solutions' process more bearable and interesting in the midst of our life's 'blue northers.'

CHAPTER ONE

INSTANT RESOLUTION

One of the most devastating soul storms Christians face today is the 'blue norther' of what I would call the desire for "instant resolution." This is a storm that leaves us vulnerable to disappointment and misunderstanding of God's concern for our well being because our dilemma is not instantly resolved when we pray. Believers must become storm-proof to this prevalent thought process.

In this day of instant gratification, we expect God to answer our questions and solve our problems instantly as well. A drama unfolds on screen and is concluded within ninety minutes, (*at least*). We have microwave ovens, quick-frozen foods, shrink-wrapping, fast oil-changing facilities along with fast food, fast cars and fast information. These and many other innovations have caused today's society to expect swift conclusions to every problem encountered.

Stress levels are rising to new heights and people are looking for fast relief. Pressures from such a fast-paced lifestyle are taking a severe toll on the well being of this world's inhabitants. Eroding morality and accessibility to fleshly temptations in our 'open society' in addition to the instability of this world's system and its changing values, have caused even believers in Christ to experience a myriad of difficulties that often seem overwhelming.

We have made great strides in medical remedies. Pharmaceutical sales of aspirin, painkillers and depression

3

fighting, mind-altering drugs are at an all time high. Man wants a "cure" *from* the pain; God wants to "cure" the *cause of* the pain.

If you are expecting God to provide "an instant fix" for your difficulties in today's world, you will oftentimes be disappointed. You *will* encounter problems. Therefore, your focus must *not* be on the problem itself but on God and His solution to that problem ~ not a solution of your own (see John 16:33).

Instant answers are not efficient ways to develop persistence and endurance in your everyday life.

Another component extremely detrimental to the resolution process is the element of wanting comfort or relief as part of the problem's solution. Sometimes there will be neither comfort nor relief. God is more interested in your character than He is your comfort.

God's remedies for your 'blue northers' (*I'll also call them problems and attacks*) is a *process* involving time, energy, discipline and faith. God's process for making us 'storm-proof' has many forms and purposes. This process seldom includes an "instant, comfortable resolution." Perhaps the most important aspect for you to remember is, that from God's perspective, the purpose of this process is to do whatever necessary, *"to conform you to the image of God's Son [Jesus Christ]."* (Romans 8:29)

You may ask, "In what ways am I not like Jesus Christ?" "What will it take to make me more like Him?" I believe the answer is the message of this book ~ the process of discovering and obeying God's way of doing and being right. *"All things work together for good for*

4

those who love God and are called according to His purpose." (Romans 8:28)

We need to realize that from God's perspective, the "good" mentioned in Romans 8:28-29 refers to the believer becoming conformed to the image of Jesus. Many times the definition of what *we* think our "good" should be is quite different from what *God's* meaning is.

This places an entirely different perspective to Romans 8:29, when observed from God's viewpoint. God's plan for your "good," consists of "what *process* will best conform *you* to Jesus' image." Instant, comfortable solutions are just not thorough enough.

The most important remedy God has for all of man's problems is that of man's eternal salvation. It is impossible to become storm-proof or seek solutions from God apart from entering into the *only* provision for man's eternal life that God has provided ~ a personal relationship with the Lord Jesus Christ.

Perhaps you are a person who has experienced difficulty in accepting and understanding God's salvation. The mystery of salvation is both simple and profound.

Jesus said *"I am the way and the truth and the life: no one comes to the Father but by [through] me."* (John 14:6)

He didn't say, "I am a way," but "the way" to the Father. It is not enough to just 'know about' Jesus, you must 'know Him' personally. Paul, in the Colossians 2:2-3 refers to God's mystery (the gospel) as Christ Himself, in

Whom are hidden all the treasures of wisdom and knowledge.

How do you get to know Jesus Christ personally? You get to know Him in the same way you get to know anyone. Spend time with them, communicating with them and enjoying their company. It is the same way with Jesus. To develop a relationship with the Lord of Life, you must find out what He likes and dislikes. The Bible is a love letter written by God to His children. Why not get intimately acquainted?

Do you know what God has to say to you, His child? Are you His child? To proceed without this decision to personally know Jesus is folly.

SALVATION

If you are one who has not made this most important decision, I invite you to *choose* now to join God's family of believers by asking Jesus to be the Lord and Savior of your life. If there is any doubt that you have made this decision earlier in your life, follow these same instructions.

Have faith (believe) that Jesus is the Son of God Who died on the cross to pay for your sin. He rose from the dead and has prepared a place for you in heaven. When you make Jesus the Lord of your life, His offer of salvation to you is entirely free. This is His grace activated by your faith in Him.

Simply say the following prayer aloud to God *from your heart*. Trust that He will hear you and answer you with His eternal assurance that you are His.

PRAYER FOR SALVATION

Father, in Jesus' Name, I ask you to come into my life and change me. I proclaim You to be Lord of my life. Cause me to be *born-again*. I know I am a sinner. I give you all of myself that I can, to all of You that I know.

I ask you to forgive me of all my sins. I believe that Jesus is the Son of God and He died on the cross to pay for my sin. I believe that Jesus rose from the dead and is with the Father interceding for me.

Please, Lord Jesus, come into my heart right now. Cleanse me and make me new. Thank You for Your grace that saves me through faith in You. I accept You as my Lord, in Jesus' precious name, A-men!

If you prayed this prayer from your heart, you are now "born-again" into the family of God. You are indeed a new creation, "born of the Spirit, washed by the blood." Congratulations!

In one respect this solution can indeed be referred to as an instant resolution.

CHAPTER TWO

DEFINING TERMS

In order to clarify statements and terms being used, this chapter will define a variety of terms used throughout this book. This is so you may have the correct understanding and greatest benefit from all that is taught herein.

THE KINGDOM OF GOD

How does one define the Kingdom of God? God's Heaven, His domain or Sovereignty, God's areas of rule, etc. are some of the synonyms used. These are all accurate to a degree, but a more simplistic definition can be found in the following verse.

"But seek (aim at and strive after) first of all His kingdom and His righteousness (His way of doing and being right), then all these things taken together will be given you besides." (Matthew 6: 33)

By substituting the phrase *"God's way of doing and being right"* in the place of the phrase *"the Kingdom of God,"* you get a better understanding of what is indicated in New Testament scripture by God's kingdom.

What *is* God's way of doing and being right?

God gave the answer to mankind after the great flood; it's the same answer that exists even through today.

"While the earth remains, seedtime and harvest, cold and heat, summer and winter, and day and night shall not cease." (Genesis 8:22)

Jesus, in several parables explained the *Kingdom of God* in terms of *sowing and reaping, seedtime and harvest.* Multiplying what is given you is another illustration from the parables of Jesus was concerning the Kingdom of God.

Sowing and reaping describes this exactly. After seeking His kingdom first (Matthew 6:33), the *things* that will be added (verses 24-32) are referring to and are certainly recognized as *your needs.* This will occur if you plant your *seeds* in the '*way God does things.*' This actually means a walk of absolute trust, belief and reliance on Him [*faith*, if you will]. Then your *harvest* [the multiplication of your seed] will result in having all needs met in Him.

By learning how to cooperate with Abba, Father in getting your needs met, you are on the track of withstanding the 'blue northers', which enter your life.

Another most fascinating facet of Jesus' teaching on sowing and reaping is the story told about wheat and tares [or darnel]. (Matthew 13:25-43) Tares (darnel) are weeds that look like wheat until they reach maturity. Weeds are defined in Mark 4:19.

"The cares and anxieties of the world and distractions of the age and the pleasure and delight and the false glamour and deceitfulness of riches and the passionate desire for other things creep in and choke and suffocate the Word, and it becomes fruitless."

9

Weeds are not something you knowingly plant and are certainly not something you want to harvest or bring to maturity. The enemy sowed them and there are certainly plenty of them to deal with.

According to Jesus' parable in Matthew, the master told his servants not to destroy the weeds unless they also might eliminate part of the wheat. The servants were instructed to wait until the maturity of the harvest and then they could easily identify the weeds. Weeds produce different fruit.

God does not want to waste any part of the seed you planted. Therefore in the parable, He told the servants to wait until maturity before destroying the weeds. This may also be true with some of the weeds growing in your life today. God may want to wait until harvest time before eliminating these weeds. Look toward the fruit (or its lack) that is being born in your life.

These weeds, which occur in your life, distract you and prevent you from reaching the full potential God intends for you.

Some of these weeds are sown through sin, unforgiveness, ignorance, disobedience and rebellion.

Note: *unforgiveness, ignorance, disobedience and rebellion are the very doorways through which Satan enters your life and also your harvests. They must not be allowed to remain open to him.*

Other weeds are sown and known as generational iniquities, unholy soul-ties, curses and bloodline connections (*I will describe these in more detail later*).

Our Lord told another parallel parable that is useful for finding meaning in *God's way of doing things*.

Mark 4:3-8 is the parable; the definitions within the parable are in Mark 4:14-20. The *seed* is the Word; the *soil* is man's heart. The *weeds* are in defined in verse 19 (listed above), the thirty, sixty and a hundred times as much as was sown has to do with *multiplying* what was sown in the heart. What is planted is the seed and it must die in order to reproduce.

"*Unless a grain of wheat falls into the earth and dies, it remains [just one grain; it never becomes more but lives] by itself alone. But if it dies, it produces many others and yields a rich harvest*". (John 12:24)

As long as you are alive (to the flesh), referred to earlier, you are committed to living as only one without producing fruit. If you die (to the flesh) the reproductive process (within the spirit) commences and you produce a rich harvest.

There are four distinct seasons in *seedtime and harvest*: 1) preparation of the *soil*, 2) *planting*, 3) *growth or maturation* and 4) *harvest* with cultivation and watering occurring as needed.

Cultivation concerns the elimination of weeds and maintaining good soil condition. Regardless of the weeds' origin, they must be eliminated and the soil's good condition maintained in order for the harvest to be optimal. The earlier in the process weeds are recognized and eliminated, the better.

The *shortest season* is the one of *harvest or reaping*. The *longest* is the *growing season*. The *most critical season* is the timeliness of *planting* (and dying), while the *most tedious season* is cultivating and watering.

According to Jesus' definition, the seed is the Word; the soil is the heart where the seed is planted, and a successful harvest depends on the correct application of the Word. Remembering these facts helps you to participate in "God's way of doing and being" (*The Kingdom of God*) more effectively.

Recall that God is the Alpha and the Omega, the Cause and the Effect, not only *the beginning and the end* but also the *'in-between'*. The seed is the Word of God. When you receive revelation of the Word, it must be planted in well-prepared, receptive soil [your heart]. The flesh must die so the seed can begin to grow, mature and multiply.

To summarize, "God's way of doing and being right." Guard the precious *seed* until your *soil* is prepared, determining through God's instruction *where* and *when* you *plant*, dying to the flesh and follow His remedies for growth and maturing. This will ensure harvests of thirty, sixty and an hundred-fold. You are charged to bear much fruit or to multiply what is given you. If you don't multiply what you have, then even what you think you have will be taken away.

One last thing, when unable to understand the ways and purposes of God, the questions of *"Why, or Why Not, God?"* are often best answered from the perspective of distance. This distance can be one of time, or it can be the distance earned only through maturity or experience.

HOLINESS

Many believers have a problem accepting the fact of their personal holiness. If you don't believe in your personal holiness before God, the winds of adversity will conquer and cripple. Problems arise because your understanding is confined to what holiness does not mean.

Consider thoughts such as the following:

"There is no way anyone, especially God, could call me holy." "My thoughts, attitude, behavior and words are certainly not descriptive of being holy." Do these phrases sound familiar? Have you thought or said them to yourself?

Holiness is *not* something you do. It is *not* something to be 'worked up' by human effort. Holiness *is* something you *believe* resulting from a *conscious choice* of yours to believe. Holiness is to become separated [sanctified] unto God.

The path to Holiness is through <u>faith</u> ~ not <u>human ability</u>!

There are no degrees of Holiness –
Only degrees of maturity in Christ!

God spoke to Moses (Exodus 3:3-4) and later to Joshua (Joshua 5:15) and said, *"Put your shoes off your feet, for the place on which you stand is holy."* This is not in reference to any particular location of acreage or dirt on the earth but indicates the condition of protecting your flesh in the Presence of God.

When you put confidence in your flesh to aid or enhance your righteousness or holiness with God, you are in error. You cannot perform at a high enough level in order to earn God's favor or reward. Flesh and its stench of self-effort cannot stand in the Presence of God. The shoes as mentioned above refer to attempts to protect your fleshly self-efforts in order to be holy.

"But I say, walk and live [habitually] in the [Holy] Spirit [responsive to and controlled and guided by the Spirit]; then you will certainly not gratify the cravings and desires of the flesh (of human nature without God). (Galatians 5:16)

It is important therefore, to lay down the sword of *good intentions*, the spear of *willpower*, and the arrows of *human resolve and effort*. Accept the 'burning bush' before you as God's fiery zeal against *all flesh* brought into His Presence masquerading as holiness or righteousness.

Accept the fact of what Jesus did for you and me on the cross. He bought and paid for our holiness. What Jesus did and what God said — *not* what *we do or think* — determines our holiness. It is part of the package of salvation.

SPIRIT, SOUL AND BODY

According to Genesis 1:26, man is created in the image of God. God is Triune [three in one]: Father, Son and Holy Spirit. Man is also triune and consists of spirit, soul and body (see 1 Thessalonians 5:23).

Understanding the distinctions and differences in the three parts of human beings will aid in the conditioning and preparation of your being able to withstand the stormy seasons. As mentioned earlier, the three parts of man are:

- The SPIRIT of man is the immortal, undying essence of man designed to have fellowship with God, with the potential of becoming co-ruler with Jesus as His bride. In the process of salvation the spirit of man is *born again* instantly and permanently. The spirit of man is the <u>Seat of Joy</u>!

- The SOUL of man makes up the man's *personality*. It too, is immortal and therefore carries your individual unique personality into your life hereafter. The soul of man is in the process of being sanctified, justified, fortified and delivered (*born again if you will*). This is why, after salvation, man is afflicted with many of the same habits and patterns of thought accompanying him/her in the 'lost' (*without Christ*) state.

  There are three parts in the soul of man. **The mind** [our logical, deductive, intellectual agency], **the will** [our volitional, elective, free-to-choose capacity] and **the emotions** [the seat of passion, place of sensitivity and emotive response center]. These make up your **soul**. Simplistic words for your soul might be: "The Thinker (*the mind*), The Feeler (*the emotions*) and The Chooser (*the will*)." Man's soul is the <u>Seat of Happiness.</u>

- The BODY of man is the *container* for man on the earth, in this natural span of life. It is inextricably connected to the other two parts but is designed to separate from them upon physical death in this natural realm. The body dies and returns to dust, the spirit and soul returns to God from Whom they originated. When we receive our glorified bodies in the hereafter our being will once again be complete and united: body, soul and spirit. The body of man is the <u>Seat of Pleasure</u>.

The SPIRIT of man is created for the worship *of* and fellowship *with* the Living God. Man's spirit was designed to receive revelation from God. Thankfulness, gratitude and praise begin with the soul but worship involves the spirit of man.

Joy, unlike happiness and pleasure, *is not* dependent on external conditions for its manifestation. *"And be not grieved and depressed, for the joy of the Lord is your strength and stronghold."* (Nehemiah 8:10)

This is why the spirit of man is called <u>the seat of joy</u>. Joy can be permanent and perpetual because it is not dependent on external conditions for its existence.

The SOUL of man is created to house the seat of man's consciousness and his freedom to choose. It is not difficult to understand that man's SOUL has become the main battlefield Satan uses to try and steal, kill and destroy mankind. *"The thief comes only in order to steal and kill and destroy."* (John 10:10)

Happiness, unlike joy but similar to pleasure, *does* depend on external conditions to allow its manifestation. Happiness is usually associated with materialism. It also depends on individual emotional stability within human relationships. The soul of man is called <u>the seat of happiness.</u>

Happiness is temporary and transitional. Pursuing happiness for happiness' sake alone creates opportunity for the enemy to influence man's decisions negatively.

Man's BODY is the temple of the Holy Spirit, created to be yielded unto and offered as a living sacrifice to God. Man in his bodily form was given the command to have dominion over the earth. Spirits without bodies were not given authority to do anything in the natural world. Evil spirits are constantly looking for bodies to allow them to exercise dominion in the earth or natural realm.

For this reason, man has the authority to 'cast out' evil and unclean spirits through Jesus Christ the Savior, Healer and Deliverer. This is also part of the Good News of the cross. When man sins with his body, he sins against the Body of Christ.

"Do you not know that your body is the temple (the very sanctuary) of the Holy Spirit Who lives within you, Who you have received [as a gift] from God? You are not your own. You were bought with a price [purchased with a preciousness and paid for, made His own]. So then, honor God and bring glory to Him in your body." (1Corinthians 6:19-20)

As <u>the seat of pleasure,</u> man's BODY contains the sensory and tactile machinery to experience and promote pleasure. Pleasure like happiness is dependent on external influence for its manifestation. Pleasure is also temporary and transitional as is happiness. The same warning expressed for seeking happiness exists for seeking pleasure just for pleasure's sake. It opens the door for demonic activity and influence.

It is God's will that the human SPIRIT, controlled by and in obedience to the Holy Spirit, dominate the SOUL and the SOUL dominate the BODY. Man's SPIRIT communes with God then gives orders to the SOUL. Man's SOUL rests in submission to his SPIRIT then obediently directs the BODY.

Man's BODY then is yielded to its functions as 1) the temple of the Holy Spirit, 2) presented as a living sacrifice, 3) yielded unto Christ as belonging to Him.

It is through this process that unity, health and maturity occurs even when facing 'blue northers.' You become storm-proof when you are not leaning on pleasure or happiness for the measure of success or satisfaction in your life. You learn to obtain and walk in the joy of the Lord at *all times*. In this way man can truly become the ruling Bride of Christ.

It is to be remembered that The Kingdom of God is not a *democratic or consensus form of government* but is instead, a *benevolent dictatorship.* We are to obey God and *not* rely on the voice of consensus, majority or just make popular decisions.

Independence from God in any part of our BODY, SOUL OR SPIRIT opens the door wide for an onslaught from the enemy. Many problems we face will be eliminated as we understand and apply this truth.

Meditate on: *"I said, I will take heed and guard my ways, that I may not sin with my tongue; I will muzzle my mouth as with a bridle while the wicked are before me."* (Psalm 39:1) *"Do not allow your mouth to cause your body to sin..."* (Ecclesiastes 5:6)

HOPE

Faith is preceded by <u>hope</u>.

"I know the thoughts and plans I have for you, says the Lord, thoughts and plans for welfare and peace and not for evil, to give you hope in your final outcome." (Jeremiah 29:11)

"Why are you cast down, O my inner self? And why should you moan over me and be disquieted within me? Hope in God and wait expectantly for Him; for I shall yet praise Him Who is the help of my countenance, and my God." (Psalm 42:11)

"Faith, hope, love abide, these three; but the greatest of these is love." (1Corinthians 13:13)

Observe some of the Biblical definitions of hope and what it has for you and me. Hope is to wait, tarry, rest and depend on God. Hope, faith and expectation are interwoven with each other. A person's outward expression is a reflection of his/her hope. To hope is to reach forward not backward!

Hope is a desire of some good, and differs from wish and desire in this, that it implies some expectation of obtaining the good desired, or the possibility of possessing it. Hope, therefore, always gives pleasure or joy; whereas wish and desire may produce or be accompanied with pain

19

and anxiety. *"The Lord will be the hope of His people."* (Joel 3:16 KJV)

Hope is an opinion or belief not amounting to certainty but grounded on substantial evidence.

Hope is the human part and *faith* is the divine part of the equation but *love* is the cement binding them together. Hope is the belief, desire, and the passion of the heart. <u>Hope becomes faith when God speaks to you personally concerning your hope.</u>

Hope will not circumvent the sovereignty of God. Just because you hope something does not guarantee God will give it to you. Faith is not taking something from God; it is to believe in, and be obedient to, something God *tells* you. Since this is true, any decision, action and/or thought (these mentioned above) without faith is not effective or pleasing to God. This is foundational to faith. A summary of faith is as follows:

FAITH

Much has been said and written concerning faith. This is not an attempt to enlarge upon these efforts but instead, to simplify into bite-sized pieces an understanding God has revealed to me that has been beneficial in my faith decisions.

To correctly understand and appropriate the *basic principle* of walking, talking and obeying God in your life, the approach must be made through *faith*. Every *decision* made, every *action* attempted, and/or the *thought processes* accompanying these activities must come from a foundation of *faith*. *"Without faith it is impossible to please God."* (Hebrews 11:6)

Each of the steps listed in this book is to be approached, understood and applied from a standpoint of *faith*.

Faith is an established boundary of God
that prevents the dream, petition,
and/or action from shrinking.

Faith is for your right standing with God!
Works are for a witness to man of
your right standing with God.

The first act of faith is trusting in the truthfulness of God. This trust will be developed through your spiritual discernment as you read and study the Word of God and listen attentively to His voice. Another act of faith is trusting in God's truthfulness concerning the 'casting out' of satanic forces in Jesus' Name. This is fulfilling God's Word in faith.

Faith is a divine substance. It can be either a fruit or a gift. A gift comes ready to use, complete in all aspects. When presented by God, a gift is to be received and used in a certain situation or circumstance.

Faith as a fruit, on the other hand is planted into your being and must be nurtured and cultivated. It does not come ready to use but rather must be grown to maturity. Then it is ready for use in the service of our Lord.

Faith comes from the Lord, Himself. When you have this first element [hope] then present it to the Lord as described in the steps below.

• **Hope.** Determine what is your hope. Hope is based on your desire or passion of your heart. *"[Now] we have this hope as a sure and steadfast anchor of the soul [it cannot slip and it cannot break down under whoever steps out upon it — a hope] that reaches farther and enters into [the very Presence] within the veil,"* (Hebrews 6:19)

Hope never gives up. You present this hope to God for Him to speak to it.

• **Hear.** You must hear God's Word (*determine if the Word you hear is of/from God*). If you do not hear God's Word concerning what you are about to do, you are walking only in your desire or your wish, and dangerously close to walking in presumption, not in faith.

All of us know that the Bible is God's Word. However, we should be reminded that *the Bible is not the total source of God's Word.* There are many ways God speaks to us.

"And there are also many other things which Jesus did. If they should be recorded one by one [in detail], I suppose that even the world itself could not contain (have room for) the books that would be written." (John 21:25)

Other examples of where you can hear God's Word are listed.

1) <u>Nature</u> declares itself as the handiwork of God and speaks messages not contained in the Bible.
2) <u>Prayers' answers,</u> i.e. *"Should I marry this person, take this job, etc."*
3) <u>Personal prophecy</u>
4) A <u>word of knowledge</u>
5) A <u>word of wisdom.</u>
6) A <u>sermon or teaching</u> where God enlightens your understanding with a rhema word ~ not necessarily a scripture verse(s).

It is important to recognize the voice of our Lord in whatever forms it manifests itself.

• **Believe.** After hearing from God, you must believe God's Word (*a conscious choice on your part*). When you have determined you have definitely heard from God, you must make a conscious choice to believe it. God's Word has been described as His truth and His promise.

   "Therefore [inheriting] the promise is the outcome of faith and depends [entirely] on faith, in order that it might be given as an act of grace..." *"Fully satisfied and assured that God was able and mighty to keep His word and to do what He had promised."* (Romans 4:16a, 21)

• **Receive.** Next, simply receive God's Word (If a Word is not received, it is not possessed). To hear and believe you have heard from God is useless unless you receive it. Sometimes you must verbally state *"Father, in Jesus' name, I receive Your Word."* Again a conscious choice must be made that the Word (promise) is yours and receive it as such.

•   **Trust.** You now must choose to trust God's Word (*confidence*). By definition, trust is total confidence in the integrity, ability and good character of another.

Your confidence in God's Word is a firm acceptance that it is true and will accomplish what He says it will do. There is always risk involved because risk is an accompanying facet of faith. The major risk you face is that you must depend on God alone, *not* someone or something else (even yourself). Realize that if you are exercising your faith in what you think God is saying and you miss Him, God is still pleased and will clarify where you have strayed. In this you must trust God.

•   **Obey.** You must be very careful to obey God's Word. Every Word of God has the condition of something to obey in it. Many times the obedience segment is to wait patiently until the answer is manifested. This is the most unpopular and most difficult form to obey.

•   **Rest.** A new revelation to me from God is to rest in God's Word (*Sabbath*). It is my belief that this rest refers to the Sabbath that is not only a particular day of the week, but is the Sabbath rest of the believer. The Sabbath of the Bible was a time of inactivity within a week's time frame.

The Sabbath rest of the believer extends to *the resting of the mind* in regards to the integrity, veracity (*habitual truth*), justice and friendship of Almighty God, Himself. It then becomes possible to rest in the assurance that God's specific Word to His child will prevail.

This rest, to my understanding, is not referring so much to a ceasing of *physical* effort in weekly work, but applies to a cessation of fleshly efforts to assist God in accomplishing the answers to petitions. It refers not merely to just a period of time ~ *Chronos* [*a Greek word meaning the passing of time as the ticks of a clock*] ~ but a season of time ~ *Kairos* [*also a Greek word meaning season*].

The resting in His Word to which I refer, consists of being at peace. This means the absence of anxiety and worry whether it is for a season or for a definite space of time.

To function in **Peace**
is to perform in/with the absence of the
distresses experienced as a result of sin.

Here's an example of faith in action. If you become aware through spiritual discernment of a satanic attack (*demonization*) upon yourself or another person, and you hope to help them/yourself become free from this attack, you must first determine what God's Word says concerning these kinds of attacks. *"And these attesting signs will accompany those who believe: in my Name they shall cast out demons."* (Mark 16:17)

From your hope, you present it to God for Him to speak to you His Word. You hear the Word; you then must believe the Word. Next, receive the Word, trust the Word, obey the Word [this is where you speak to the demon in Jesus' Name, bind it and its influence on the person/yourself and cast it out]. You then rest in the Word [have confidence the Word or promise will accomplish what is intended]. You can now thank and praise the Lord for His victory.

Another example is when you know of someone who is sick, compassion in your heart prompts a desire (or hope) to see this person become healed. You ask God how He wants to heal this person and wait for His Word concerning this healing. [This is where we encounter difficulty because you sometimes only obey what *you* want to see accomplished, rather than ask God what He wants.]

After hearing a positive answer from *God's Word*, in *obedience* to what the Word directs, you lay hands on the person, perhaps anointing them with oil, offering up a prayer of faith for their healing.

During this time you *believe* what God's Word says, *receive* the meaning of the word, *trust* His Word, and then *obey* the Word (if there are further instructions). After this you merely *rest* (or remain at peace) in the Word letting God's grace perform His purpose in this exercise.

Your faith must *never* be directed toward the desired *results* of your hope, but *only* toward the grace provided by the Author and the Finisher of your *faith*, even the Lord Jesus Christ.

"Therefore [inheriting] the promise is the outcome of faith and depends [entirely] on faith, in order that it might be given as an act of grace." (Romans 4:16)

Thus, placing faith in the Author and Finisher of your faith, instead of a desired result, allows you to obtain the inheritance of the promise that is yours because of the inheritance of the promise that is yours because of God's Grace. You are a participant but the results are totally His.

Behold a solution to your soul storms!

CHAPTER THREE

QUESTIONING GOD

Many of us have yet unanswered questions that we have asked of God. This is quite normal. God tells us His ways are not our ways and His thoughts are not our thoughts (see Isaiah 55:8). There will always be many things of God we will not understand. The problem arises when these questions degenerate into reasons for doubting and unbelief in God and His love. This is especially pertinent when facing tragedy and calamity. Thus enters another 'blue norther' from which we need to be insulated.

Never throw away what you know to be true because of something you don't understand!

When a friend, loved one or even you suffers, thorny questions often arise. Many believers are at a loss as to how to answer or be of comfort. Unfortunately, there are no 'pat' answers. There are almost as many answers as there are problems. Sometimes there is only an assurance of God's Presence rather than a definitive answer. Ask God to reveal Himself and/or give an answer that will comfort and give peace. Trust Him to do this. Remember, "Never throw away what you know to be true because of something you don't understand!" Just because something you believe in and trust for doesn't happen, you must never let that cause you to stop believing in God.

Another answer to the inevitable question of "Where was God when this or that particular thing happened?" is this: "God was in the same place He was and has the same concern when the religious leaders abused, mocked and killed His Son, Jesus."

Psalms 29:10 gives us a great word of encouragement, *"The Lord sat as King over the deluge; the Lord [still] sits as King [and] forever."* The deluge mentioned refers to the great flood, and God sat as King during it.

Whatever is happening or *not* happening in your life, God still sits as King and will continue forever. There may be no definitive answer to this particular problem facing you this side of glory, but God still reigns and you can trust Him.

Let me share a question I had with God and our consequent conversation on a particular subject.

GOD'S LOVE

Not long after I became a 'sold-out' believer in Jesus, I was learning the truth that I could be completely honest with God. Not only was He Savior, Deliverer and Healer to me, He became my Abba, (the Hebrew word for daddy). I was asking Him (in all honesty) how it is possible for me to love Him with all my heart to the exclusion of my wife, Joyce and our two girls, Norma and Versia.

The conversation went something like this: "Abba, how do You really expect me to love you more than my wife and my girls? My daughters are the products of a marriage between two people who love each other so much that these two fine girls are the result. I felt them move in Joyce's stomach, watched them both come into this world at birth, heard their first cries and observed and participated with their growth into the sweet young ladies they have now become. That's just the way I feel about the girls, Abba."

"With Joyce, I can't conceive having more or deeper love for anyone than I have for her. You gave her to me. We fit together. She has seen me at my best, my worst and all the in-between's. She still loves me in spite of my shortcomings, my lapses in attention, my ill-chosen words, and my moodiness. How do You really expect to compete with love such as that?"

Very gently and with as much attention to my request as possible Abba answered. "My son, I am the essence, the very center and source of love. Everything you feel for Joyce, Norma and Versia came from *My* heart. I also was there when all the things you mentioned as important to you occurred. I rejoiced with you in all parts of what you describe. Love is not just a feeling it's a choice, too. If you choose to love them more than you choose to love Me, <u>you will be limited to loving them with all *your* heart</u>. But if you will choose to love Me first and deepest, then <u>you can love your wife and daughters (yes, and even others) to the limitlessness of *My* heart</u>."

"If anyone comes to Me and does not hate his [own] father and mother [in the sense of indifference to or relative disregard for them in comparison with his attitude toward God] and [likewise] his wife and children and brothers and sisters — [yes] and even his own life also — he cannot be My disciple." (Luke 14:26)

I then understood that God wasn't commanding something for me to do that was *not* beneficial for me. But by my obedience, I could be greatly enriched. Rather than having something taken away, His limitlessness was being added. So it is with all God's Words.

THE TRUTH

Another time I was asking God to show me about His truth and how I could contain it all. I was shown a very large metal pot filled with liquid ~ I was reminded of the cartoon strips depicting a pot that was big enough for cannibals to cook missionaries in, that's how large it was!

On this big metal pot there were handles of metal that looked like large coffee cup handles approximately two feet apart located all around the upper edge.

God told me the liquid contained in the pot represented His truth. He then told me to pick up the pot. Obviously, after studying it, I realized the impossibility of my strength being sufficient to lift it. I also saw my reach was only wide enough to reach over about three or four of these many handles. This would result in my tipping over the pot even if I did have the strength to lift my side of it.

Wisely, I told God that I was not strong enough, besides even if I was strong enough, I would tip it over, and spill some of it. God then told me I was correct. "All of My truth is too heavy for one person to handle. It becomes necessary for each member in the Body of Christ to lay hold on the handles before him and by all of you lifting together, you can handle and dispense all the truth without spilling it."

The conclusion to the 'what is God's truth' question is ~ I need you and you need me so we can all share all the truth God has for all of us in His body. I believe this little prayer will aid the reader in resolving some of these kind of nagging questions.

Abba, help my questions to You be those that are based on trust in You. Deliver me from questions that arise from doubt and unbelief.

Just as an adult son talking with his father asks questions — let my questions to You be based on confidence and trust, never from doubt and unbelief.
In Jesus' Name!

There are of course, times when a believer feels abandoned by God. There is no apparent sense of contact with Him in any area of life. Frustration, fear, defeat, disappointment, etc. have set in. This is not unusual!

At other times we go through fiery ordeals of pain, disillusionment and conflict. Again, this is not unusual! Consider this:

"Beloved, do not be amazed and bewildered at the fiery ordeal which is taking place to test your quality, as though something strange (unusual and alien to you and your position) were befalling you. But insofar as you are sharing Christ's suffering, rejoice, so that when His glory [full of radiance and splendor] is revealed, you may also rejoice with triumph [exultantly]." (1Peter 4:12-13)

Does any of the above pain sound familiar to you? Has the cold wind and destroying ice of a 'blue norther' frozen out your trust and dependence on God? Regardless of what you find yourself going through, it is considerably less than that which Jesus endured for us.

Do you feel rejected? So was Jesus. Do you feel disappointed? So did He. Have your friends, loved ones, associates and/or leaders despised you and your efforts? Much more so did they despise Jesus. Do you feel abandoned by God the Father? Jesus suffered through all of that on our behalf. He finally gave his life as a substitute price for all the sins of the whole world ~ past, present and future. His was the only sacrifice God the Father deemed sufficient and satisfactory for sin's penalty.

The key word for us to think on and carry with us during times like these can be found in Psalms 23. *"Yes though I walk through the [deep, sunless] valley of the shadow of death, I will fear or dread no evil, for You are with me; Your rod [to protect] and Your staff [to guide], they comfort me."*

Yes, you're going to walk *through* valleys of death. You will not *escape* them but you will *not* remain *in* them. With faith in the living God you will *choose not to fear* because He is *with* you. He *will* protect and guide you.

There is a song sung by Ron Kenoly called "Go Ahead." The first line of the lyrics is very appropriate to our discussion. It is, *"If you catch hell, don't hold it. If you're going through hell, don't stop."*

You must not hold on to the hell you catch here on earth and when you find yourself going through a hell, you must not stop.

You must not hold on to the hell you catch here on earth and when you find yourself going through a hell, you must not stop.

These thoughts have been of great comfort to me in my times of fire. My wish is that they will be of comfort also to you when you find yourself in the midst of a valley of the shadow of death. May these thoughts also equip you with the courage to stand when there is nothing else you can do. May they give you the guts to trust the outcome to the only One Who is worthy of your trust and Who loves you enough to give you the correct answer, the Lord God Almighty.

One such stormy occurrence I was facing some time ago I'll describe to you. One of our daughters (both of whom are very dear to us), in her turbulent teens would not embrace the gospel or accept Jesus as her Savior and Lord.

We did all we knew to do. We argued and debated, we prayed and fasted. We saw nothing to indicate she was any closer to the kingdom.

During one Saturday morning in which I was travailing for her, the Lord dropped these words into my heart while I was waiting before Him. I share them with you if you have a similar burden that they may be of comfort to you as well.

My dear one:

You have sought My face and My will concerning this loved one in your life. I tell you now by My mouth that cannot lie, this one for whom you are praying and interceding is not far from the Kingdom of God. She seems to be taking a long time coming into My kingdom but you are not to be anxious or fret because of the length of time. I am the God of time and I am in control of all circumstances.

As you are praying, you are being made to become mighty in faith and strong in prayer and intercession. Your prayers allow Me to work in the loved one's life, but also allows Me to do a mighty work in your life as well. I am pleased with your effort and motivation and have thus spoken this word to encourage you to continue to seek Me. Continue to read My Word more thoroughly, to increase both the quality and quantity of your prayer time with Me.

I am answering the prayer of My Son, the Lord Jesus Christ Who prayed for you described in John's gospel. "You are not of the world but I will keep you from the world and protect you from the world and the evil one. I will sanctify, purify, consecrate and separate you for Myself to make you holy."

I will make you holy by revealing the truth about what I see in your soul. Yield and release to Me, this that I reveal to you, to be removed from you so you can be made holy as I am holy. Only in holiness can there be oneness with Me.

I am speaking My Word to you and I will accomplish My Word in you. Peace be with you. My peace I leave with you!

Abba

Within a year from then, our daughter was gloriously and permanently saved. It is my hope this can be an encouragement for someone who is perhaps facing a similar situation.

God does not mind if you ask questions. Questions and their answers allow us to discover truth and gain better understanding of most things facing us. When answers are not forthcoming or understanding is not readily available in the circumstances in which you find yourself, you must then rely on faith in God and His character. You can endure anything if you know that God, with His character of love, compassion, mercy and grace, is walking through this situation *with* you. It is good to remind ourselves of this fact often.

If you understand God wants you to trust and obey Him for *your* benefit, not *His*, you can begin to have the right perspective in *all* his remedies. This will take you farther along the pathway to a storm-proof walk in the presence of 'stormy weather.'

CHAPTER FOUR

TYPES and ORIGINS of ATTACKS

Where do attacks originate?

All Christians experience problems (soul storms) which confront them. These problems originate from a variety of sources. The following descriptions of various problems, their points of origin and related attacks will be of help as you proceed through the book.

The more understanding you can have for difficulties that you face, the more prepared you can be *when* they occur.

Problem Solving

I watched a brother experiencing a problem one day and became quite disturbed at the way he was <u>not</u> handling it. It seemed he was approaching it from the wrong viewpoint, jumping to the wrong conclusion and expending a lot of unnecessary effort, with little improvement in the situation. He did not ask my advice nor was I impressed to offer it. However, from my viewpoint, I was sure I had a better solution. I was fussing over these observations when the Lord spoke to me in my spirit.

He showed me a huge, hand-cut diamond approximately four feet high and maybe three feet in diameter. Its sides were expertly cut and shaped so the sparkle and refraction were exquisite. God then said to me, "How many sides are there in this stone?" I replied, "I

don't know but You do, Father." He said, "Yes, I do!
Now how many of those various sides face you?" I told
Him, "Only one, Sir." He said, "Very good. Now
remember there are various sides and facets to every
problem man faces, but there is only one side of the
problem that faces you. Face and address only that one."

That admonition has been very helpful when I begin
to tackle my problems or see those of others.

When we look for the sources of attacks, we need to
realize that Satan has specific goals for any and all
demonic assignments.

Satan's *primary* goal or directive is to keep a person
from surrendering his/her life to the Lord Jesus Christ.
Once Divine salvation makes that goal impossible, Satan's
second goal is to keep the believer, by whatever means
possible, from embracing and walking in the abundant life
offered by Jesus. This is where many of the storms in our
lives originate.

If Satan can keep you trying to 'fix' side(s) of the
problem that don't face you, he has you occupied in doing
things that are *not your tasks*. This will exhaust your
energy and misdirect your focus from the things on which
God wants you to concentrate.

*"The thief comes only in order to steal and kill and
destroy, I came that they may have and enjoy life, and have
it in abundance (to the full, till it overflows)."* (John 10:10)

Knowledge of God and His ways comes by
revelation to the spirit of man rather than from information
gained through man's mind (soul).

"Now we have not received the spirit [that belongs to] the world, but the [Holy] Spirit Who is from God, [given to us] that we might realize and comprehend and appreciate the gifts [of divine favor and blessing so freely and lavishly] bestowed on us by God. And we are setting these truths forth in words not taught by human wisdom but taught by the [Holy] Spirit, combining and interpreting spiritual truths with spiritual language [to those who possess the Holy Spirit]." (1Corinthians 2:12)

Where do man's problems come from?

The problems faced by mankind originate from at least four arenas.

1. The supernatural or spiritual realm
2. The natural realm
3. Personal arena [*those problems affecting you*]
4. Non-personal arena [*all other problems including other persons, situations and circumstances*]

Let us examine them individually.

1. The supernatural or spiritual realm

This arena is the higher level of existence in which, as the name implies, resides the supernatural or spiritual realm.

This is sometimes referred to as the invisible realm. It is untouched by our natural laws, which relate to time and space. There are both good and evil forces existing in the supernatural realm. Because the demonic forces are related to the fallen angels, much demonic activity affecting you has its origin in this arena.

A problem or attack which originates in the supernatural realm is one which is not produced according to the ordinary or established laws of natural things ~ a miraculous event, if you will. Witchcraft draws upon evil supernatural power to achieve its desired results, while prayer calls upon the unlimited power of God.

2. The natural realm

The natural realm is the current plane of existence we are experiencing today. It is subject to all the natural laws of physics, space and time. When a natural situation (problem or attack) occurs, it has a natural cause and corresponding natural effect or consequence. When problems occur in this realm there will be natural explanations (accidents, illnesses and natural disasters are examples). Having said this, when a problem occurs it is still a problem even if you *know* the explanation for it.

3. The personal realm

The term "personal" refers to problems or attacks that are originating within and unto you, affecting your immediate situation or you <u>personally</u>. These can be problems concerning your finances, your relationships, your health, and your personal fulfillment (or satisfaction) in your vocation (or avocation), etc. From this arena you find your objectivity to be very limited while your "blind spots" become uncommonly numerous. "You can't see the forest for the trees."

In this arena, you are often in need of someone other than yourself to assist you. Any part of your person can be affected, i.e. your physical body, your mind, will or emotions. Many times you are limited in what you can discern personally because you are so intimately involved.

This is when and why we need each other. Others can more objectively observe your "blind spots" and help prescribe viable solutions.

4. The non-personal realm

This arena refers to other problems, situations and circumstances not covered in the above mentioned areas. These can be problems or attacks occurring with other individuals, groups, communities and/or nations. These problems may also affect any area from catastrophic to political.

Note: *In the last two arenas (the personal and non-personal realms) the problems' <u>origination point</u> will be either natural or supernatural or a combination of both.*

Attacks (Problems)

It is a fair assessment to state that a problem is an attack and an attack is a problem. Therefore, the two terms are used interchangeably and have reference to the storms or 'blue northers' mentioned earlier. These are the items in which, from an endurance or overcoming standpoint, you are to become "storm-proof."

There are three general classifications of problems / attacks, (3-S's) Sin, Self and Satanic. There are also three

41

solutions or remedies for them, (3-C's) Confess, Crucify and Cast Out. These are listed below in the correct order of attack/problem vs. appropriate solution:

- for a <u>Sin problem you must Confess the sin to God</u>

- for a <u>Self-problem you must Crucify the flesh</u>

- for the <u>Satanic problem there must be a Casting out of the demon(s)</u>.

The appropriate remedy must be applied to the associated cause to be effective, i.e. *you cannot cast out 'Self' or cast out 'Sin' ...you can only cast out 'Satan'*.

Let me compare the solutions of these problems to using a tool from a toolbox. I have a toolbox at home containing several of the most necessary tools for 'fixing' things that need repair. If my lawnmower's carburetor needs adjusting, I don't use the claw hammer. Likewise, I don't use the screwdriver to drive nails. I use the correct tool for the task. The same is true using our spiritual tools for spiritual problems.

Remembering that our warfare is not with flesh and blood, spiritual weapons (or tools), not natural ones are the correct tools to use.

To reduce all problems/attacks with their associated difficulties into three categories appears to be over-simplistic. The truth is, when reduced to their basic origins which are the causes of our problems or attacks, there are only the three possible areas. These three can occur in any one of the major areas mentioned earlier: the supernatural, the natural, the personal or the non-personal realms. This book is written from this premise.

A. Sin problems

What does the term sin problem mean? Sin is defined as an action, thought, word or behavior that separates you from God. These are based upon the precepts contained in the Ten Commandments and the teachings of Jesus.

When you have a sin problem, whatever you are tempted by most will be the focused area of the attack.

Perhaps, as an example, you are most tempted by lust. Satan certainly knows you have that problem, and his attack will be in that area.

When our Lord went to the cross and paid the price for all the sins of the whole world, you and I were given the avenue through which we can be forgiven. That avenue is confession or agreement with God.

"If we confess our sins, God is faithful and just to forgive us our sins and cleanse us from all unrighteousness." (1John 1:9)

Confession is the cure or remedy for sin. We must confess and receive forgiveness and cleansing by faith. It is *real*, it is *true* and it is *available* to you personally, anytime and anywhere. For this reason, confession is to be embraced and not avoided.

Why is it necessary to confess and repent of sins?

To Confess to God in the sense used here, is simply to verbally agree with God and what He says sin means in terms of separation from Him (see 1John, chapters 1&2). Of course you are not telling God something He does not already know.   You are instead, *coming into agreement* with Him as to the nature and seriousness of the offense (sin) committed or omitted.

Implied is the term **Repentance.** Repentance is to change the mind from one idea or direction to another idea or direction. It means to turn from sin and error to forgiveness and truth.   Repentance also requires a conscious change of choices. To repeat,

If you have a sin problem confess the sin.

B. Self problems

The flesh is the part of you that wants to be comfortable at any cost.   It is more than just creature comforts and includes all parts of the soulish realm (*see Body, Soul and Spirit explanation in Chapter 3).*

The flesh is merely wanting to be 'in charge' or 'in control' in all the areas of your life ~ a 'self' problem, if you will.

"Unless a grain of wheat falls into the earth and dies, it remains [just one grain; it never becomes more but lives] by itself alone. But if it dies, it produces many others and yields a rich harvest. Anyone who loves his life loses it, but anyone who hates his life in this world will

keep it to life eternal. [Whoever has no love for, no concern for, no regard for his life here on earth, but despises it, preserves his life forever and ever.]" (John 12: 24-25)

This explains the need of death for the one (self), so Christ can produce a harvest of many from our lives. Failure to die to self prevents the replication leading to multiplied life through Christ living within you. You must die in order for Him to live. To die to self is to reproduce the abundant life of Jesus the Christ.

"... If anyone intends to come after Me. Let him deny himself [forget, ignore, disown and lose sight of himself and his own interests] and take up his cross, and [joining Me as a disciple and siding with My party] follow with Me [continually, cleaving steadfastly to Me]." (Mark 8:34)

"And those who belong to Christ Jesus (the Messiah) have crucified the flesh (the godless human nature) with its passions and appetites and desires." (Galatians 5:24)

You might ask, what does Jesus mean when He says *"take up your cross daily and follow me?"* The cross to which Jesus is referring has been described as anything or anyone you are holding in higher esteem or importance than Christ. That person or thing that is so valued by you is the cross upon which you must die. The flesh must die, and the only way that can be accomplished is to crucify the flesh in that area.

How do you know that you are operating 'in the flesh?'

There is a definitive answer to this.

"Now the doing (practices) of the flesh are clear (obvious); they are immorality, impurity, indecency, idolatry, sorcery, enmity, strife, jealousy, anger (ill-temper), selfishness, divisions (dissentions), party spirit (factions, sects with peculiar opinions, heresies), envy, drunkenness, carousing, and the like. I warn you beforehand, just as I did previously, that those who do such things shall not inherit the kingdom of God." (Galatians 5:19-21)

What does it mean to crucify the flesh?

To Crucify the Flesh simply means to act contrary to and deny what the flesh desires or demands (the opposites to the above list). To crucify the flesh is to say 'yes' to the Holy Spirit's decisions to the exclusion of what the flesh does or does not want.

When your problem is of a *fleshly nature*, the attack will be in or toward a weakened area of your flesh. 'Flesh' is identified as any area of the soul [*thinker, feeler, and chooser*] as well as bodily appetites and addictions.

This is a large and complex arena that includes man's health from a physical, mental and emotional perspective.

In the case of addictions, medical science can sometimes aid the process. [*If you use medicine to the exclusion of scriptural principles, you have treated the symptoms and ignored the cause. Likewise, using a scriptural approach while omitting known scientific methods is ignoring the advantages God has granted to man through the discovery process*].

If you are tempted to look in a video store with pornographic videos, you must avoid the travel path taking you beside or near that store. It becomes necessary for you (*by crucifying the flesh*) to alter your willful behavior in avoiding an area of temptation.

Another example is this; an unemployed recovering alcoholic does not need to get a job as a bartender.

Still another example is in the area of ministry. Care must be exercised when counseling someone of the opposite sex one-on-one or in a private situation apart from others. Many have been seduced by their own flesh to succumb to its desires concerning someone of the opposite sex with whom they are ministering.

Crucifying the flesh also has a further identification with the fellowship of Jesus' suffering at the crucifixion.

Crucifying the flesh must be consistent and continuous in order to keep the flesh from obtaining control in your life.

Believers must be lead by the spirit man, obeying the instructions from the Holy Spirit of God, resulting in control of both the soul and the body being yielded to the spirit's (Spirit's) decisions.

To repeat:

If you have a Self problem Crucify the flesh.

C. Satanic problems

There is a battle raging between the Kingdoms of Light and Darkness for the right to rule over the human life. Both the Lord and Satan ask the question, "follow me". The final choice is yours as to who is to be lord of your life.

If the life has been surrendered to Jesus as Savior and Lord, the battle is only in the soul and will of man. The adversary uses your sins, weaknesses, ignorance and disobedience as doorways through which to enter into your life. Satan is a legalist. Therefore, he cannot enter or use his influence in any area not legally open to him.

As stated above, most of the battle from the satanic realm is in the mind or emotions (*the soul*). Scripture depicts the devil thusly,

"...For that enemy of yours, the devil, roams around like a lion roaring [in fierce hunger], seeking someone to seize upon and devour." (1Peter 5:8)

According to Jesus' words in Mark 16, you have authority to drive out (cast out) demons.

"And these attesting signs will accompany those who believe: In My name they will drive out demons; they will speak in new languages; they will pick up serpents; and even if they drink anything deadly, it will not hurt them; they will lay hands on the sick, and they will get well."(Mark 16:17-18)

Describe what casting out the devil means!

To cast out has to do with using the weapons of Spiritual Warfare, under the direction of the Holy Spirit to recognize, address and subdue demonic activity.

Some of the weapons to be used in Spiritual Warfare are: 1) The Name of Jesus, 2) The blood of Jesus, 3) The breaking of curses and iniquities, 4) The breaking of unholy soul-ties, 5) Breaking the power of unforgiveness.

The conclusion is that under the authority of the Name of Jesus, the kingdom of darkness is driven or cast out.

A "filling up" of the vessel must follow the act of casting out demons. The doorways open to sin must also be shut.

"When the unclean spirit has gone out of a person, it roams through the waterless places in search [of a place] of rest (release, refreshment, ease); and finding none it says, I will go back to my house from which I came. And when it arrives, it finds [the place] swept and put in order and furnished and decorated. And it goes and brings other spirits, seven [of them], more evil than itself, and they enter in, settle down, and dwell there; and the last state of that person is worse than the first."
(Luke 11:24-26)

The "filling up" needs to be with the Fruit of the Spirit and/or that trait, which is the opposite of what was cast out. It must be remembered that in the case of the born-again believer, you are dealing not with the spirit of man but, rather his <u>soul</u> [thinker, feeler and chooser] and/or his <u>body</u>.

I have many different ideas of submission. What does submission really mean?

<u>Submission</u> is defined as "*allowing* the person or object to which you are submitting, to be who or what they are in authority or position." Submission is an attitude that transcends behavior. This will clarify passages such as these found in James 4 and Ephesians 5.

"*Submit yourselves therefore to God, resist the devil and he will flee from you.*" (James 4:7)

"*Wives, be subject (be submissive and adapt) yourselves to your own husbands as [a service] to the Lord.*" (Ephesians 5:22)

When attacks occur upon the <u>Body</u> or upon the <u>Soul</u> (thinker, feeler or chooser (*see Chapter 3 Body, Soul and Spirit explanation)*, ask yourself the following:

- Am I being attacked because of some <u>unconfessed sin</u> in my life? God is faithful and will tell of unconfessed sin if I just ask Him.

- Is the attack due to <u>disobedience</u> in some form? Is the attack a consequence of some bad or evil habit? Is it because of verbal agreement with something that is contrary to God's Word? Can this attack be caused by <u>compromise</u> to what the Word of God states? What was the last thing God told me to do, and did I do it?

- Is the attack due to something in an area where I am *weak*? Have I been told about this and failed to exercise the options where I have been instructed? Is <u>negligence or ignorance</u> a factor in this?

- Is this attack caused by any generational, genetic or ancestral <u>curses</u>?

Depending upon the answers to the above questions, you can determine the correct pathway to a solution. Remember the attacks can originate in the supernatural realm but will always manifest in the natural realm. The solution will begin in the natural but through faith will unfold in the supernatural (invisible), resulting in the manifestation of the solution in the natural realm. 1Corinthians 15:46 states, *"But it is not the spiritual life which came first, but the physical and then the spiritual."*

Correct solutions come after the identity of the attack/problem is determined and its purpose and origin are disclosed.

To summarize:

> *If you have a **sin** problem, **confess** the sin.*

> *If you have a **self** problem, **crucify** the flesh.*

> *If you have a **satanic** problem, **cast it out.***

CHAPTER FIVE

ROOT CAUSES & ASSOCIATED ATTACKS

Believers in Jesus Christ, aware of the existence of problems that confront them, often wonder where these problems originate. This chapter will review the root or basic types of problems and their various related attacks. Just to identify a malady is insufficient without a viable solution to it. These solutions are God's way of making you "storm-proof" in the soul storm's attempt to destroy you.

Although the items described are applicable for all mankind, the emphasis will be on identifying and solving these problems and attacks <u>from a believer's perspective.</u>

God's Solutions and Treatments

God has a solution to and a treatment for any problem or 'blue norther' you face. That is certainly good news! However, one of His solutions is not so popular; it is the solution of "<u>Just endure My child</u>." Sometimes God's answer <u>to wait</u> comes because of the need for more time to correct another area of your life or someone else's life before solving this problem. God sometimes allows attacks to occur or continue to expose 'blind spots' previously hidden to you. God will offend your mind for you to discover what is in your heart.

What actions are detrimental to the solution of my problems? What is the correct solution for my problem?

The uncertainty you encounter is often because you don't want to make the situation worse by a wrong response. When trying to determine the answer to the above questions beware of two negative reactions: denial and rationalization in all forms.

Denying that the problem exists is *folly,* while rationalization trying to portray the problem in some socially or personally acceptable term is *deception.* Both reactions are extremely harmful to finding a true and lasting solution.

Call your problem exactly what it is! (It's a sin, or it's my flesh, or it's a satanic attack, not a 'my personality disorder,' 'my dysfunctional environment' or 'an alternative life style,' etc.) Correctly identify what the problem really *is* and *is not.*

Accept the *responsibility* for *your own decisions* and *choices* rather than trying to affix *blame on someone or something else.* This course of honesty will be the first step toward confession of your sin or of dealing with issues of your flesh.

Attacks occur in specific problem areas. These were introduced in a previous chapter. When it's a **sin** problem, **confess** it to God. When it's a **self** problem, **crucify** the flesh and when it's a **satanic** problem, **cast** it out.

Treatment of Problems

When a problem (attack or 'blue norther') exists, it must be treated and cured, else it becomes worse and spreads. Some solutions to problems consist of healing and deliverance.

Healing and deliverance can be used interchangeably and can refer to either a **"hygienic"** or a **"therapeutic"** process. Both methods are effective and beneficial when used properly.

What does the term hygienic healing or cleansing mean?

By *hygienic healing or cleansing*, I mean *maintaining* the healthful cleanliness provided through *habitual* cleansing. There is a type of "uncleanness" that occurs in the physical realm because of activity and neglect. The reason we brush our teeth, or wash our hands or take baths is to maintain a status of cleanliness (or prevent uncleanness) due to our activity. To *not* do this is to invite an afflicted state of health with accompanying disease and infection.
The same rationale exists for the spiritual well-being of individuals.

There is a *hygienic* standpoint in maintaining good spiritual health as well. Certain activities to which believers are exposed cause an accumulation of uncleanness, which needs to be habitually and methodically cleansed.

Working in an environment of worldly values day-by-day where bad language, pressure and stress leave their residue of negative influence on a believer. This begs for the cleansing power of forgiveness (*i.e. brushing the teeth*) on a regular, periodic basis. There is also the condition of unconfessed sins that have crept in unobtrusively or overtly over the course of a day's work. These need to be confessed to a loving Father (*i.e. washing the hands*).

Women who find themselves overworked and exhausted tending to the duties of a wife, mother, 'go-fer', housekeeper, employee, etc., find themselves sinking into the mire of self-pity, despair and discouragement.

Believers (*both men and women*) of all classes suffer from this daily contamination in the world. A need of periodic cleansing (*i.e. daily baths*) from these downward spirals is necessary for good mental, emotional and spiritual health. This is what I call *hygienic healing or cleansing*.

Daily prayer, Bible reading and time alone with God are good examples of this type cleansing. When you get alone with God, His Holy Spirit will indeed convict you of areas in your life in need of *hygienic* cleansing and healing.

Describe therapeutic deliverance and healing or cleansing!

Therapeutic healing or deliverance refers to another medical term denoting a process of recovery. This is remedial healing and cleansing when the injury was severe and somewhat isolated in nature. There is always accompanying pain with therapy. This pain, unlike symptomatic pain indicating alarm and warning, is now indicative of recovery. It is to be expected and embraced so as to see it diminish with restoration of health. You have to learn to re-use the affected part that was injured.

To illustrate, when a traumatic injury is so severe that a limb must be immobilized to allow proper healing; the recovery process after the surgical procedure has a follow-up of physical therapy.

When a child breaks an arm in a fall, and the arm has to have emergency trauma intervention, it then is placed in a cast for several weeks. The muscles of the arm deteriorate during its convalescence. The initial pain of the injury is indeed different from the pain of re-setting the broken bone. Now there is pain associated with its becoming healed. Upon the removal of the cast an intensive program of rehabilitation called physical therapy begins. It is a slow but progressive process filled with a different type of pain that results in the restored use of the arm. In the same way, after a severe spiritual wounding (and its associated pain) a process of healing or cleansing (with its different type of pain accompanying) is needed. This process is of necessity focused on the specific area of injury to provide relief and recovery through the pain.

Some forms of deliverance and healing are similar to the example above. There is the need for a process of slow but progressive recovery from a deep, initial spiritual, mental or emotional wounding. This most often occurs through an in-depth understanding of who you are in Christ Jesus, how much you are loved, accepted and approved by the Father, allowing you to become free from the bondage and captivity of the rejection and bitterness which caused the wounding.

Treatment varies according to need and severity; some treatment is *remedial* and some is for *maintenance and/or prevention.*

The Bones Which You Have Broken

For example, shepherds mentioned in the Bible were amazing people who possessed wisdom, stamina and perseverance. A good shepherd understood how to truly train and discipline his sheep. They were called by name and responded only to the shepherd's voice.

Because sheep are not known for being very sharp animals, sometime stringent measures were employed to assure compliance with the shepherd's wishes.

The parable told by Jesus in Luke 15:4-7 illustrates part of this point. The shepherd lost one sheep out of the one hundred in his care.

When a sheep was lost, the shepherd would take all means at his disposal to recover it. However, if a sheep continually wandered away from the flock and other efforts failed, the shepherd would break the bone in one of the straying sheep's legs. Then he would set it and bind it so healing would take place.

In the six weeks or so that it would take for mending to occur, the sheep could not move on its own. Food, water and rest for the sheep were in the shepherd's hands.

Because of the broken leg, the sheep was not allowed to leave the shepherd's side and even when the flock moved, he rode around on the shepherd's neck and shoulders.

During this time the sheep learned that by staying close to his master he was completely satisfied. By listening to his master's every command and feeding on what is supplied by his loving shepherd, who calls him by name, wandering away is no longer an option he chooses. After the healing is completed the sheep never strays away from the shepherd again.

When King David had strayed (much as the wayward sheep spoken of above) and separated himself from God, Yahweh confronted him through the prophet Nathan. Nathan accused David of the sins of adultery with Bathsheba and the murder of her husband Uriah. David confessed the facts and during a season of true repentance wrote one of the most familiar psalms, Psalm 51.

> Note: *The loss of David and Bathsheba's baby was their punishment. Also David was not allowed to build the temple because of the blood that was on his hands. However, Solomon, the son of Bathsheba and David was the one chosen to build the great temple.*

Now, to the remaining point of the story. In the psalm, David asked God for *"mercy"*, *"washing from his iniquity and guilt,"* also *"take not Your Holy Spirit from me"* and *"Create in me a clean heart, O God."* David also implores God in verse 8. *"Make me to hear joy and gladness and be satisfied; let the bones which You have broken rejoice."*

David, a shepherd in his youth, remembered how a stubborn, wayward sheep must be disciplined. He knew the value of the broken bones in his life, which were necessary to keep him close to his Master. David, like the sheep, never again strayed from his Lord in Whom his needs were always met. His relationship with His God never wavered again. He could truly say, *"The Lord is my Shepherd, I shall not lack (or be in want)."* (Psalm 23:1)

This true story illustrates more accurately how therapeutic healing can occur. God sometimes allows pain that you despise in order to mold in you the thing He loves, your obedience.

The Importance of Diagnosis and Obedience

Treatment of the problem begins with a correct diagnosis. There can be no withstanding of the storms in your life without learning to recognize and correctly treat your susceptibility and weaknesses to attack. By this I mean get to the root (basic cause) of the problem.

Is the problem you face one that you (or someone else) acquired through periodic infection and uncleanness, or has this malady occurred because of a deep and severe wounding? In either case the answer is usually sin in one form or another. Sometime the sin is *committed* and at other times it is sin resulting from something *omitted*.

This can be *your* thoughts, words and/or actions or they can be the thoughts, words and/or actions of *another*. The cause or origin of sin may be from any one or a combination of all three areas mentioned above: sin, self, or satanic.

Don't be guilty of basing the diagnosis upon human reasoning, logic and/or knowledge. Only God can see into man's heart and know his motivation. A human can be easily fooled. If the wrong diagnosis is drawn and treatment is made toward the wrong source, only the devil will be pleased with the results. The Holy Spirit must show the correct diagnosis to you. Ask Him!

After correct diagnosis, there must be obedience. Unlike diagnosis, this obedience *can* be executed within the boundaries of human knowledge and experience. By using principles in God's Word concerning the diagnosis, obey what the scripture states. If the symptoms reveal unforgiveness, bitterness, resentfulness, etc., then read what the scripture says regarding how to respond to those areas. Ask God to show and confirm the diagnosis. Then obey the Holy Spirit's prompting.

An obedient heart will embrace the use of **Confession of sin(s)** and **Repentance**. These were covered in chapter 2, but bear repeating here.

Confession of sin to God is to agree with what God says concerning the sin that is causing separation from Him. Call it exactly what it is and spare no ugly details. In faith, accept Jesus' death on the cross as sufficient payment for the sin and receive forgiveness for it.

Repentance is to 'change the mind' or 'change directions.' It means to turn away *from* something *toward* something else which are more profitable or beneficial for you.

Identify specifically *by name* the individual sin revealed to you by the conviction of the Holy Spirit.

Confess this sin to God. Renounce and turn away (repent) from it. Begin this as a verbally stated *choice* then follow-up with appropriate *action*.

Repentance will do several things for you. It will remove the legal rights of the devil to practice chaos in that area of influence in your life. When legal rights are *restored* to you as a believer, You have the authority and right to exercise dominion in all areas of your life subject to the rule of the Lord Jesus Christ. Repentance also provides an open door through which recovery can occur through medicine, deliverance or other such processes.

Forgiveness

One of the 'blue northers' often used by Satan to defeat and devastate you is the storm of *unforgiveness*. Without exception every believer has to effectively deal with this 'crippler of man' in order to stand erect and be insulated from its destructiveness.

When approaching the topic of forgiveness, one issue has to do with the forgiveness of your personal sin(s). Only God can do that. This is what Jesus accomplished by dying on the cross. He paid the penalty Father God required for the payment of not only your sin(s), but also the sin of the whole world.

To appropriate this forgiveness of your sins(s) you must confess the sins, repent of the sins, ask God to forgive you of the sins in the Name of Jesus (*appropriating the payment Jesus made on the cross for sin*) then receive the forgiveness of your sin(s) in faith.

The other approach to forgiveness is that of <u>forgiving others</u> for how they have offended you. This type forgiveness can sometimes be defined as "<u>Breaking the Power of Unforgiveness</u>" in your life and is the subject of this discussion.

All have experienced rejection in some form within their lifetime. The Bible speaks at length about the need for you to enter into forgiveness from such rejection.

"The purpose of forgiveness is so we can reverently fear and worship the Living God." (Psalm 130:4)

Your 'fear' of God is sometimes only a 'dread' or a 'terror' of God, and you find yourself unable to properly enter into the worship of our Lord when under the power of unforgiveness.

<u>Forgiveness</u> breaks the power of resentment, bitterness and ill will present in your life. It restores you to the cleanliness and peace necessary for you to truly fear and worship God as you are designed to do. The fear of the Lord as described in the Bible is fear combined with love, not the fear of terror or dread.

In Matthew 18:23-35 Jesus relates a parable illustrating the kingdom of heaven (*God's way of doing and being right*) as it pertains to *forgiveness*. In it He speaks of a servant of a king who owed the king a debt of millions. When the king demanded payment the servant asked the king to have patience with him and he would pay everything. The king's heart was moved by compassion and he forgave the servant of all he owed, canceling the debt.

The same servant as he went out, met his fellow servant who owed him a twenty-dollar debt. He demanded immediate payment and was met with the same plea he had given to the king, "Give me time and I will pay it all."

Being unwilling to do this, the servant put his fellow servant in prison until he paid all the debt.

When the king found out what had happened, he called the servant into his presence and confronted him. "I forgave you and cancelled all that great debt of yours because you begged me to. And should you not have had pity on your fellow attendant, as I had pity and mercy on you?" And in wrath the master turned him over to the torturers (the jailers), till he should pay all that he owed.

Here is the commandment Jesus gave: *"So also my heavenly Father will deal with everyone of you if you do not freely forgive your brother from your heart his offenses."* (Matthew 18:35)

This gives both the command and the consequences of disobedience for *unforgiveness*.

The Lord does not give a command that cannot be obeyed!

There is another command given by Jesus that is often overlooked. It emphasizes by scripture how repentance and forgiveness proceed hand in hand. Our Lord said just before He ascended, *"... repentance [with a view to and as a condition of] forgiveness of sins should be preached in His Name to all nations, beginning from Jerusalem."* (Luke 24:47)

From this passage it appears that *repentance* is also a condition of *forgiveness.* Recall what the meaning of repentance is, *to feel such regret over (an action, intention, etc.) as to change one's mind.*

When seeking forgiveness for <u>personal</u> offenses you must examine yourself and feel the regret you have caused the Father then 'choose' to change your mind (*repent*) concerning this.

When seeking to forgive <u>others</u> for offenses against you, the repentance is on *their side* of the issue. You must repent of *your* intentions, thoughts, words, actions, reactions, etc. You cannot repent for *someone else.*

You are given the tool of forgiveness to be used with and in the **Name of the Lord Jesus Christ** (*not in your name or any other name but His*). This is an act of faith and may explain why some cannot find the power within themselves to forgive. They are thinking they must have personal power to forgive the act(s) rather than asking and acting in faith toward God.

A few persons feel they can only forgive if they are the ones who are "at fault." It is not necessary to know the 'at fault' person or situation. It is only necessary to know that our Lord says to *forgive regardless* of the *at fault* factor. If you are involved in an offense and/or its accompanying hurt, you are *commanded* to forgive.

Some also think that in order to forgive, you <u>must also forget.</u> Forgiveness is not evidenced or confirmed by *spiritual amnesia.* Forgiveness instead allows *healing in the memories* so that recalling the event of offense does not result in the recurrence of the emotional hurt associated with the original act. True forgiveness can only come through and by the power of that special Name, "JESUS."

Forgiveness must be exercised in the following areas in order to be effective: <u>Person(s)</u>, the <u>Situation or Circumstance</u>, <u>Myself</u> and <u>God</u>.

- **The Person(s)** who were was responsible for the offense's occurrence. *Their awareness of this offense is not a factor.* When a <u>person</u> is responsible or blamed for an offense a <u>person must be forgiven</u>.

- **The Situation or Circumstance** deemed responsible for the offense's occurrence. For example, you may find it necessary, if you feel resentment or inferiority, to *forgive* the fact (*circumstance or situation*) that you were born *who* you are, the *way* you are, *when* and *where* you were born if your ethnic or racial background or your physical characteristics, etc. are an issue. When a <u>situation or circumstance</u> is *responsible or blamed* for an offense the <u>situation or circumstance must be forgiven.</u>

- **Yourself** - for receiving an offense and/or reacting as you did to it. (*Your guilt or innocence is not a factor*). This is especially true when you find *fault* or *blame* in yourself for an offense occurring. I am not talking about condemnation but conviction of guilt (*see conviction and condemnation explained below*). When you *blame* yourself, <u>you must forgive yourself.</u>

- **God** - to whatever degree you *blamed* Him, either for *not* changing the situation, *not* stopping the offense or *allowing* it to proceed. Many *never* feel they are blaming God. But when the person, situation or circumstance created an offense and God did nothing about it, you sometimes subconsciously *blame* Him. It seems strange, but you may need to <u>forgive God to whatever extent you blamed Him.</u>

As you may have suspected, there may be the need to exercise *forgiveness* in more than one of the above-mentioned areas to be completely free from the influence of the offense. Most offenses have more than one overlapping area of *blame or fault* that cause *unforgiveness*.

Since offenses in our lives are a constant and ongoing process, forgiveness must be a constant and ongoing process as well. There will be very few days in which something or someone does not cause an offense and needs our 'forgiveness muscle' to be exercised.

The "R & A" Factor

Another necessary step you can take to follow the Lord's command concerning forgiveness is what I call the 'R&A' factor. Again this must be enacted in faith.

The 'R&A' factor refers to "<u>Receiving and Accepting</u>." You must choose to <u>receive and accept the person or the situation in the same way the Lord Jesus Christ receives and accepts them.</u>

This does not mean you were wrong and the person(s) doing the offending were right, or even what was done to you was right and you were wrong to take it as you did. That's exclusively and only God's job. The R&A factor means you don't have to be judge or avenger.

You may find yourself receiving and accepting any one or a combination of the four factors mentioned above "as the Lord Jesus Christ receives and accepts them." This simply puts you in the position of agreeing with God regarding what He says concerning what happened to you and those who offended.

By taking this step you also find yourself getting out of the way of God's revenge. You have no right to the *"get even"* attitude offered to you by Satan. *"Vengeance is Mine, says the Lord."* (Deuteronomy 32:35) This position of agreement with how Jesus receives and accepts one who offends is a position of freedom and peace for you.

Many concentrate only in selected areas of forgiveness (mostly areas of human effort), leaving something lacking in your freedom and peace. This may explain some of the reasons you have difficulty exercising this most important commandment of our Lord to forgive.

You are invited to use this sample prayer and embrace any needed areas of unforgiveness in your life.

PRAYER FOR BREAKING
THE POWER OF UNFORGIVENESS

Father, I forgive ____*(from the list)* in Jesus' Name For __ *(fill in personal details of the offense)___*.   I now receive and accept _ *(from list)_* as the Lord Jesus Christ receives and accepts *(him, her, myself, them, and/or it).* I thank You Father that it is done, In Jesus' matchless Name.

When discussing <u>confession of sins to God,</u> <u>repentance from sin and/or forgiveness</u>, it becomes necessary to understand one of the most potent 'blue norther' weapons used by Satan. Satan cannot create but he does counterfeit many of the things of God. This formidable weapon is <u>condemnation</u> or <u>false guilt,</u> which is Satan's counterfeit of <u>conviction by the Holy Spirit</u>.

Conviction and Condemnation

<u>False guilt</u> and <u>real guilt</u> feel almost identical. In the same feeling way, <u>condemnation</u> relates emotionally to <u>conviction</u>. They are however, very different. Because of the similarity in emotional feelings between the two, it is often difficult to distinguish the differences between them. The following comparison will help explain these differences.

What is the difference in conviction and condemnation?

- **Conviction** is *always* from the Holy Spirit, *never* from Satan. Many times, when you may feel embarrassed about what is revealed concerning your actions or attitude, you want to blame Satan. It may in reality be conviction by the Holy Spirit. Conviction always addresses an action or attitude never you or your character. You must discern the *basis* of things revealed to you.

- **Condemnation** is *always* from self or Satan, *never* from God. Sometimes there is self-condemnation as well as condemnation from the devil. Condemnation always attacks you or your character. Analyze your 'self-talk', what are you saying to yourself concerning this problem? Where is it coming from?

- **Conviction** is very *definite* and *specific* in what is to be corrected. It is direct and precise so you will know exactly what must be fixed. You may be convicted of gossiping with another person.

  Conviction presents a solution that is recognizable and do-able. This overlaps with the preceding point and reveals an obtainable conclusion. The Holy Spirit, in His conviction to you will specifically tell you to quit gossiping. You then must confess it as sin, repent, and then ask forgiveness of the one who was offended.

- **Condemnation** is *indefinite* and *vague* in details of what is to be corrected. There will be no clear-cut answer or direction to be taken for a remedy. Condemnation presents a solution that is imaginary and often impossible. When you feel rejected by someone's comment, your self-talk might say to you, *"You know they are right, you'll never be any different. Accept the fact you are sub-par."* If you agree with this attitude suggested, you will be under condemnation, pure and simple.

- A 'first reaction' of *denial, anger and/or rationalization* will often arise when first confronted by **conviction.** (*Satan will make sure of this*). When you have one of these reactions (*denial, anger or rationalization*), pause and ask yourself, *"Is this really conviction concerning an area of my life prompted by the Holy Spirit?"* The answer oftentimes will be "yes." Observe your 'first reaction.' If you become angry and begin rationalizing as to why you did it or begin blaming someone else for it, etc. — investigate to see if it is conviction from the Holy Spirit. <u>Failure in this area of 'first reaction' can thwart God's remedy for a sin in your life.</u>

- A <u>'first reaction'</u> to **condemnation** is often <u>agreement with the condemning argument and with its description of what you are as a result of your action, thought or deed.</u> This can be resolved by asking *"Is this really like me?" "Is it a sin I can confess?" "Is the Holy Spirit convicting me in this area?"* Observe your 'first reaction.' If you agree with the accusation, feeling shame and irreversible sorrow — suspect that it is **condemnation**. If you disagree, deny or rationalize — investigate to see if it is **conviction** by the Holy Spirit. Granted, these reactions are exactly opposite to what they should be, but the devil works very hard to get us to react according to what I have described.

- **Conviction's** conditions, when obeyed, will result in soul pain relief. All situations resulting in conviction or condemnation will have soul pain associated with them. Obedience to conviction's conditions will result in relief from this soul pain, offering peace in its stead.

- **Condemnation** has no condition for relief of soul pain, which often intensifies. Will this have a solution to relieve or lessen my soul pain?

- **Conviction** will always draw you *closer* to God. This is a final checkpoint, are you being drawn closer to God or does this drive you further away from Him?

- **Condemnation** drives you *further* from God. Again, are you being drawn closer to God or driven further from Him?

A person's 'first reaction' to accusation is a very interesting observation. It is, in most cases, the opposite of the correct action. You should *agree* with the Holy Spirit's conviction of actions, thoughts or words that have transpired. Conversely, you should *deny* and *resist* the condemnation offered by your flesh or Satan.

Instead, you resist, deny, grow angry and rationalize your guilt of *which you should stand convicted,* while you sometimes readily agree with condemnation with *which you should not agree.*

Condemnation need not be a plague to the believer. Consider this most assuring scripture:

"By this we shall come to know (perceive, recognize and understand) that we are of the Truth, and can reassure (quiet, conciliate, and pacify) our hearts in His presence, whenever our hearts in [tormenting] self-accusation make us feel guilty and condemn us. [For we are in God's hands.] For He is above and greater than our consciences (our hearts), and He knows (perceives and understands) everything [nothing is hidden from Him]. And beloved, if our consciences (our hearts) do not accuse us [if they do not make us feel guilty and condemn us], we have confidence (complete assurance and boldness) before God" (1John 3:19-21)

God is greater than our hearts, Halleluia!

How should I handle and respond to criticism when it comes?

When (*not if, but when*) criticism, censure or rebuke occurs in your life, begin to yield to the Holy Spirit's power of <u>conviction</u> if anything in the statement, action, etc. relates to the <u>truth</u>. Ask yourself, *"Is anything about this the <u>truth</u>?"* or *"What is <u>true</u> in any of this?"* Upon determining the answers, separate the truth and only the truth, then relegate the rest of the criticism, censure or rebuke to condemnation, and/or selfish, worldly or erroneous perspective.

"The ear that listens to reproof [that leads to or gives] life will remain among the wise. He who refuses and ignores instruction and correction despises himself, but he who heeds reproof gets understanding. The reverent and worshipful fear of the Lord brings instruction in Wisdom, and humility comes before honor." (Proverbs 15:30-33; 10:17)

When criticized, follow these steps:

1. Listen to the <u>entire message</u>.

2. <u>Gage your initial reaction to it.</u> Did you agree too quickly or did you react with anger, denial or rationalization?

3. Yield to the Holy Spirit for His <u>conviction </u>of what is true.

4. After determining <u>what is true, deal correctly with it</u> (*i.e. confesses sin, crucify flesh, cast out Satan*).

5. <u>Assign the rest</u> of the message (*that not true*) to:

- Erroneous perspective from someone's part

- Selfishness in some form

- Worldly values

- Condemnation (*self or satanic*)

The first step in problem solving is discovering there is a problem. When the existence of a soul storm is uncovered, the first step to its solution has begun. You must now ask God for the origin or cause of it. By continuing to ask God to reveal sources and solutions of problems or storms you are facing, you can become "storm-proof" to them.

CHAPTER SIX

GOD'S REPAIR KIT

When I worked as Director of Training in a large fast oil-change franchise, we were learning the ancillary sales advantage of repairing rock chips in automobile windshields. Part of the training program included a well-stocked repair kit.

The kit contained various items necessary for repairing the rock chips in an automotive windshield. Liquid resin, polishing resin, plastic curing squares, extra drill bits and a set of single-edged razor blades for scraping the finished repair were some of the supplies.

Included in the equipment was a high-speed drill and a mirror to be placed inside with suction cups, so the technician could see the center of the crack while working on the vehicle from the outside. There was also a vacuum pump for the evacuation of air pressure to aid the liquid resin to flow into all the recesses of the crack or chip. Finally, there was an applicator for injecting the liquid resin into the drilled out chip or crack and an ultraviolet light for curing the liquid resin to a solid.

Proper training included the following:
- diagnosis and repair of each type chip.
- ensuring the technician understood how to address the customer's concern for the rock chip and its potential danger to his/her vision and safety.

- the technician was also instructed how to inform the customer regarding the extent of the repair in both time and money.
- and, not the least of importance, the correct and timely use by the technician, of the equipment and supplies in the repair kit.

When these elements were done correctly, a badly damaged windshield could be repaired and returned to the satisfied customer with a minimum amount of time and expense, as well as making a profit for the company.

God also has a training program for His children. He, too, provides us with a solution for facing and overcoming the damaging effects of soul storms (or 'blue northers'). He furnishes us with a repair kit completely stocked with necessary supplies.

This repair kit contains education and knowledge for the proper diagnosis of the chips or cracks, along with appropriate tools for various problem areas encountered. There is even time for 'hands-on' training.

Similar to the above 'rock chip' example, we as believers find ourselves as both technicians-in-training to make repairs for *others,* as well as being customers in need of repairs.

In this chapter, I will share some of the items God provides in His training program and repair kit for use in becoming *Storm-Proof rather than Storm-Free* from the *soul storms* we are encountering.

Some of the items may be very familiar, while others may provide a new insight in finding the correct remedy for a particular problem. Perhaps the most important item in the repair kit is the ability to <u>hear from God</u>.

How do you know it is God speaking to you?

Much has been said and written concerning how to hear from God. I will add only the following. You recognize God's voice by:

- The <u>approach</u> He makes. By what avenue did you receive this word? What were the circumstances when you heard it? Circumstances serve as guideposts pointing out your true needs. Faith sees through the circumstances unto God. See God first, then look at the circumstances. Beware of reversing the order.

- By the <u>relevance</u> of what He says. How does this word apply in relevance to your way of living? Does this relate to something that you have been previously told by God to do? Is this word possibly for someone else?

- By the <u>content</u> of what He says. Does this agree with Scripture? Does it sound like what God would say? Is it encouraging and focused?

- By the <u>results</u> His words produce in you. Does it bring life, light and peace? Are you drawn closer to God and/or become a better person by obedience to this word?

Knowing that the Father accepts you means you don't have to *perform up to a standard* for God's approval. Instead, you obey because you know you are accepted in

Christ. This certainly has an effect on your willingness to hear from God.

Sometimes the voice of God *is not* easily recognized in places or things. You may find yourself like the prophet Elijah in 1Kings 19.

After a great victory through God, in which he slew 450 prophets of the god Baal and 400 prophets of the goddess Asherah before the whole assembly of Israel and King Ahab atop mount Caramel, Elijah fled to a cave to hide. God showed Himself to be the only true God before all Israel, but because Jezebel became angry with Elijah and swore to cut off his head, Elijah ran in fear some eighty miles and hid himself in a cave.

God told Elijah to go stand on the mount before God. "*And behold, the Lord passed by, and a great and strong wind rent the mountains and broke in pieces the rocks before the Lord, but the Lord was not in the wind; and after the wind an earthquake, but the Lord was not in the earthquake; and after the earthquake a fire, but the Lord was not in the fire; and after the fire [a sound of gentle stillness and] a still, small voice.*" (1Kings 19:11,12)

After hearing God's voice, in which God showed Elijah his successor and his eminent departure from this world, Elijah was no longer frightened or confused. He had his assignment and purpose shown to him, knowing God was with him in all things. Elijah could not hear God's voice in the spectacular or the vigorous, but only in *a sound of gentle stillness.*

God will speak to you, but you must listen for His voice and become fine-tuned and receptive to His frequency and volume (or lack of it).

If you are unable to hear from your source (God), you are totally at the mercy of Satan and his kingdom of darkness. Therefore, 1) you must stay attached to the vine (Jesus), 2) feed regularly from the spiritual food table (the Bible), 3) walk in the power and inspiration of the Comforter (Holy Spirit), and 4) stay in constant communication with Abba (prayer). This makes you sensitive and receptive to God's voice and His desires for you, regardless of His manner of communication.

God's desire for you must be sought *before* you proceed into any spiritual battle with the enemy. God's voice will direct you through all the traps and snares set for you, thereby ensuring victory over the devil.

"Christians motivated by God's love and acceptance are secure and joyfully obedient children. Those motivated by desire to gain God's approval are fearful and legalistic. Both groups may look the same from the outside but their hearts are in far different places."

John Wimber

Another piece of inventory in God's repair kit is called Resisting the devil.

How do I resist the devil?

James 4:7 tells us to *"Submit yourselves therefore to God. Resist the devil, and he will flee from you."* This passage is quite familiar and the quoting of it sometimes results in overlooking a very important element. Most hear the segment about *'resisting the devil' and 'he will flee from you'* but skim over the part concerning *'submitting to God.'*

To submit is to yield to the authority, power and control of another; to permit or allow the person (*submitted to*) to be what or who their title or position says they are. If you submit to God, (*yield authority allowing God to be God*) then you can successfully resist the devil. This means not trusting or relying in your own insight or understanding (Proverbs 3:5-6) when facing decisions; but to lean on, trust in, and rely on (*submit to*) God.

Resisting means to oppose and withstand another. To resist the enemy is to act, think, behave and choose contrary to what he is dictating to you.

You now have God's promise that at this point [*your submission to God plus your contrary actions to the enemy's decrees*] the devil will now flee from you. This is the desired condition in which a believer should find himself or herself.

When dealing with demonization you ask and receive positive answers to the following questions: "To whom or what are you submitting and trusting in for victory in this area?" "Are you acting contrary to, or in accordance with the dictates of the enemy?"

Proverbs 11:9 speaks to the value of discernment, *"With his mouth the godless man destroys his neighbor, but through knowledge and superior discernment shall the righteous be delivered."* Connect this statement above to the revelation found in 1John 4:1, *"Beloved, do not put faith in every spirit, but prove (test) the spirits to discover whether they proceed from God; for many false prophets have gone forth into the world."* These passages show the value of discerning and proving the spirits.

Resisting the devil also consists of what you choose and/or that with which you agree. This is based upon with whose voice you agree. Do you agree to follow the desires and dictates (voices) of Satan, your flesh and soul; or do you choose and agree instead to follow the prompting of the Holy Spirit?

Amos 3:3 warns of this dangerous activity, *"Do two walk together unless they agree to do so?"* With what or whom you agree is where you walk. This has to do with walking *contrary* to the devil's way. It also reinforces the importance of the battle for man's choices between God and Satan.

Have you ever noticed that when the devil comes to you trying to tempt you, he asks questions? These are almost always questions that call for a 'yes' or 'no' answer. "Are you really committing a sin when you do (or think) this?" "Don't you think you deserve a little slack?" "After all, haven't you been working pretty hard lately?" The devil does it this way because he wants you to answer in <u>agreement</u> with *him*. If he can get you to agree with him, according to Amos 3:3 above, you will then walk with what he suggests and wants.

> Relying on natural knowledge of facts alone is not sufficient for determining if the current spirits being confronted are from God. It takes the voice of the Holy Spirit speaking to your attentive spirit [*superior discernment*] to arrive at the truth.

Scripture admonishes you to submit to God *first* and *before* doing anything else. Choose your behavior and thoughts very carefully, making sure they are in agreement with what God wants you to do and think. Then you place yourself in position to effectively battle the enemy. These passages also indicate the necessity for you to examine and test with whom and with what you are *agreeing* before you proceed.

Just as the chip or crack can return, more extensively, in the windshield if it is not filled with the proper resin, so too can our souls be overwhelmed with evil after they have been cleansed, if we do not fill them with the proper spiritual resin.

The next item in God's repair kit is called filling the house.

What does 'filling the house' mean?

Filling the house means *refilling* man's soul with the assurance of your salvation. This does not mean being saved again. That is a "once and for all" experience, if it is genuine. However, our soul — mind, will and emotions — is in need of continual regeneration. The fruit of the Spirit is also to be used to 'fill the house' and of course, 'fill the house' with the Holy Spirit Himself.

If the house is full of the knowledge of who you are in Christ, the devil's lies to the contrary will be defeated. If the house is full of the fruit of the Holy Spirit it cannot receive the counterfeit fruit. If the house has been refilled with the Person of the Holy Spirit there will be no room for other influences. The Holy Spirit provides power to defeat the enemy in your life. Remember God's redemption and renewal changes the heart of man.

As stated earlier, Satan cannot create. He chooses only to counterfeit, mock and [steal, kill and destroy] that which God has created. All demonic influences are counterfeits of God's created virtues. Therefore, you need to know the nature of each fruit being manifested in order to determine which 'root' spirit is present. This will be of great value after the root spirit has been cast out. By knowing the virtue opposite the root spirit, you may also now accurately and effectively "fill the house."

Scripture describes the heart of man in this way, *"The heart is deceitful above all things, and it is exceedingly perverse and corrupt and severely, mortally sick! Who can know it [perceive, understand, be acquainted with his own heart and mind]? I the Lord search the mind. I try the heart even to give to every man according to his ways, according to the fruit of his doings."* (Jeremiah 17:9-10)

Jesus speaks of the heart and its fullness in Matthew, *"For out of the fullness (the overflow, the superabundance) of the heart the mouth speaks."* (Matthew 12:34b)

Jeremiah gives God's description of man's heart without Him. Jesus' words in Matthew indicate the heart of man will be full of something. Therefore, after casting out evil, the heart must be filled (or refilled) with Jesus' righteousness.

Knowledge and Education are other inventory items in the repair kit God provides. There is *knowledge* in various areas needing attention. There is *education* in the use and application of the knowledge. Exercising knowledge will help you discern if the spirits are *good or bad*.

How do you recognize good and bad spirits?

All spirits mentioned in the Bible are referring in some way to breath, air and breeze, but also are referred to as life, anger, perception, understanding (with a reference to ghost - supernatural), life ~ hence, a spirit. The Hebrew and Greek texts agree in meaning as to spirits. There are both good and evil spirits in the supernatural realm.

Each person on this earth is assigned a guardian angel to care for and accompany him or her through this life. (Psalms 91: 11-12, Acts 12:15) In like manner, Satan also assigns an evil spirit to accompany each person and to influence him or her into evil; it is known as the familiar spirit (*I'll cover this spirit a bit later*).

Evil spirits are intelligent, supernatural beings with all characteristics in use to accomplish their evil purposes. They walk, speak, hear, see, obey, seek, think, know and dwell. They are not subject to the laws of this natural realm. There are various rankings and authority and power of spirits. A 'root' spirit is more powerful and of higher rank and authority than lesser ones.

Jesus dealt only with root or main spirits. He listened, observed and discerned evil symptoms. He bound and called out the strong man then cast him out. These are good guidelines for you to follow when dealing with demonization as well.

What about having conversations with evil spirits?

There is only one instance where Jesus 'conversed with an evil spirit' by asking its name. *"My name is Legion: for we are many."* was its answer recorded in Mark 5:9.

I believe Jesus conversed with him in order to teach his disciples concerning multiple assignments of demons in a person, and not for the purpose of identifying what kind of demon was in the person. In any case, Jesus did not converse with evil and unclean spirits. He only commanded them. He discerned their presence and with a word, cast them out.

I feel this should also be *our* pattern. Conversing with demons can result in several negative things in my opinion.

First, it will make you subject to, and expose you to what a demon states or declares. Since the devil is the father of lies, his demons would try to lead you away from the truth. This could expose you to *"giving attention to deluding and seducing spirits and doctrines that demons teach."* (1Timothy 4:1)

If a demon speaks to you, you are obliged to discern whether it is the truth being spoken or a lie, innuendo or half-truth.

Another negative aspect of conversing with a demon is the time element. When you are engaged in conversation with a demon you can be sidetracked into areas and actions that will consume great amounts of time in expelling them and their fruit. This is unprofitable and can steal your time in pursuits other than those for which God has called you to engage.

Where do you send evil spirits you cast out?

When you cast out evil spirits, I feel you are to send them to "the place where Jesus sent evil and unclean spirits." There may not be clear scriptural reference as to where this might be but we know He sent them somewhere and that it was an appropriate place for them. My wife and I both, when casting out evil spirits merely state, *"In Jesus' Name, I send you to the place where Jesus sent evil and unclean spirits."*

God will never over-ride man's will, nor does He allow Satan to over-ride it as well. The will of man then becomes the prized goal of both God and Satan; therefore a constant battle rages over the choices man makes.

As a result, the greatest power man has is the *power of choice.* But he does not have the power to choose *the consequences* of his choices.

The repair kit provided by God must be maintained and kept supplied for it to function as it is designed. Once you know it is available, it is to be used frequently and consistently. Repairs are to be made to worn and defective areas of your life ~ areas such as renewing of the mind, confessing sin, forgiveness of others, etc. ~ in order to keep you *storm proof* in the center of the 'blue northers' you are experiencing.

CHAPTER SEVEN

GOD'S ARMOR AND WEAPONS

The next item in the approach to becoming storm-proof in the middle of soul storms is a multi-functional one. It has many pieces but they are to be employed as a unit; it is called the <u>armor and weapons of God</u>.

How can you use God's armor correctly?

Ephesians 6:12-18, indicates that your fight is not against flesh and blood but against despotisms (absolute tyrants, rulers), powers and master spirits who are the world rulers of this present darkness. You war against spiritual forces of wickedness in the heavenly (supernatural) realm.

This is very important: <u>Your problem is not with people</u>!

You are no match for the devil if you attempt to combat him with *natural* weapons. These would be those of human reasoning, strategy or logic. It is the devil's purpose to trap you into fighting in this way. He will always win if you do so.

Your only effective defense is the armor of God. Not only has God provided the effective defense, He has prepared a suitable offense as well. The offense against the kingdom of darkness is the proper use of God's spiritual weapons.

Both the offensive and defensive components in your warfare are dependent on the **"Nothing — Everything"** concept of faith. You are *nothing by yourself* and yet *everything in Christ Jesus.*

The armor listed in Ephesians 6:12-18 is as follows:

- The Belt of Truth to combat the deception of lies. Lies and half-truths are devastating to you, the believer, both from what you hear and what you say. The belt about the loins had special significance to the first century believer. The belt held up the robe so that the man could move agilely in crisis situations. The word loins referred to the reproductive area of the body. You are to reproduce truth in your life. Your ability to recognize and reproduce truth must be protected.

- The Breastplate of Righteousness (integrity) to battle the sludge of sin. Once you know who you are in Christ, you suffer no condemnation due to sins for which you have been forgiven. You are now in right standing (*righteous, if you will*) with the Lord.

- The Shoes of Peace to resist the onslaught of strife, confusion and unrest. All through your life, as a believer in Jesus, you will encounter strife, pressure, conflict and the like. With your feet shod in the shoes of peace, your walk will be one of peace, and you will become a peacemaker to all those around you.

- The Shield of Faith used to quench the flaming missiles of the enemy. The missiles of verbal slander and thoughts that produce shame will be neutralized. When doubt and unbelief arise and try to defeat you, you have the large shield of faith to dispel the lies of doubt with truth, peace and righteousness.

- The Helmet of Salvation to contend with the depression and despair of hopelessness. A person without hope is indeed helpless and ineffective in the kingdom of God. The quiet and absolutely settled issue of salvation defeats the condition of hopelessness and despair, thereby giving rise to active faith for combating all the schemes of the devil.

- The Sword of the Spirit (the Word of God) wielded against all the schemes of the enemy. To wield means to handle with skill and command control over. It is only as you, the believer, take up this powerful weapon of God's Word that you can become victorious over the enemy. The Word of God is to be treated as necessary to the believer as is nourishment to sustain the human body. Without it you perish. Using the sword of the Spirit the victorious believer can discover and dispense the effectiveness of truth, righteousness, peace, salvation and faith in standing against the enemy.

- Prayer is to be overall and at all times and in all seasons. It is to be constant and persistent, specific and enduring. Since prayer means communication with God, it is essential that you also make petitions to, and receive answers from our Abba Father. The one element of effective praying is obedience to what God says and doesn't say. One other vital use of prayer is to petition, in Jesus' Name, for the armor of God to be applied to you and to your loved ones. There is no stronger prayer than one of a spouse for a spouse or a parent for a child or a child for a parent.

Paul says it well: *"For this reason, I bow my knees before the Father, from whom every family in heaven and on earth derives its name, that He would grant you, according to the riches of His glory, to be strengthened with power through His Spirit and the inner man; so that Christ may dwell in your hearts through faith; and that you, being rooted and grounded in love, may be able to comprehend with all the saints which is the breadth and length and height and depth, and to know the love of Christ which surpasses knowledge, that you may be filled up to all the fullness of God. Now to Him who is able to do exceeding abundantly beyond all that we ask or think, according to the power that works within us, to Him be the glory in the church and in Christ Jesus to all generations forever and ever. Amen — so be it."* (Ephesians 3:14-21 NASB)

Putting on the armor of God consists of conscious decisions based on faith *and* knowledge - faith in who God says you are and knowledge of what and Who Scripture says God *is*. These are conscious decisions made in each of the above areas based on knowledge of what Scripture declares about each piece of the armor.

For example, when putting on the breastplate of righteousness, consciously decide and declare: "I am made the righteousness of God in Christ Jesus, therefore there is now no condemnation in Christ Jesus. I am no longer under the bondage of sin because of what Jesus paid for my sin on the cross."

Each piece of the armor increases its effectiveness with use. The more you use it the more effective it becomes.

You and I are to put on the complete armor of God *"that you may be able to resist and stand your ground on the evil day [of danger], and having done all [the crisis demands], to stand [firmly in your place]."* (Ephesians 6:13)

There is one little piece of instruction occurring in this scripture that needs strong emphasis. *"... Having done all the crisis demands, to stand firmly in your place."* Every crisis faced has something to be done in it. Something you must do. Then God will do what only He will do.

If you take the position (*in your crisis*) that you can solve or resolve it, God withdraws and lets you attempt to do it with accompanying disaster. Your response should be to make sure you have confessed and repented of all known sin, closed all sin doors open to the enemy, put on the armor then call on God to fight for you.

Many times God's fight for you consists of revelation knowledge as to the root spirit that is spearheading the attack against you with instruction of when and how to cast it out. There may be a specific sin or problem with your flesh that God puts His finger on and says, "Fix it!" Your response then is to obey the orders given you from the Holy Spirit. By submitting to God, you then work in concert (*or harmony*) with Him learning how to effectively resist and deal with the bondage of tormenting evil spirits (*or other such crisis*). (Not a bad piece of equipment to make repairs and/or prevent damage is it?)

The next item is also very effective; it is simply called God's weapons.

How do God's weapons help you?

The weapons of God, like the armor of God are not in the natural realm but are spiritual and mighty before God for the pulling down of strongholds.

What does this mean, "..*the pulling down of strongholds*"?

Strongholds were places of safety and security, impervious to assault or being overthrown. In 2 Corinthians 10, Paul compared these fortresses to places in our minds, calling them strongholds.

These are sometimes secret hide-a-ways of unholy fleshly thoughts, desires or fantasies that you fail to completely surrender to God's cleansing power. Here dwell the fantasies of fleshly desires, covetousness, envy, rebellion and jealousy. Strongholds often contain carnal passions unchecked and protected from the outside world, hopefully hidden from God so you will not receive His conviction of them. Secret addictions and private ungodly thoughts, entertained to the point of temptation, also describe mental strongholds. Each person must search his heart and mind while listening to the Holy Spirit and 'fill in the personal blanks' concerning the things just listed.

Mankind is drawn by the weakness created in Adam's fall to secretly possess something forbidden then try to hide it from God. (*Sound familiar?*) There has been little change in the devil's modus operandi (*his lies resulting in temptation*) and man's response since Adam.

Jesus Christ is the answer to defeating these strongholds of the mind. Therefore, we must initiate the process by taking these unholy thoughts into captivity.

How do you "..*take thoughts captive into the obedience of Christ*"?

This process, to me, consists of several steps.

- Identifying that the thought is from your *stronghold(s)*. **Honesty** in the discovery of just exactly what a thought *is*, and *is not*, is of paramount importance in a solution. Thoughts are just like transmission frequencies circulating in the airways from radio and television. Your mind is like a receiver. When a thought enters your mind, determine if it is from the Holy Spirit, from you, your flesh, the world or directly from the enemy. If an evil or unholy thought is from within you, it can be proceeding from one of your strongholds (*You will usually know for certain*).

- Once you have correctly identified that this is a stronghold thought, you must **choose not to entertain it**. Immediately choose to recall a scripture or a Christian song whose lyrics will relieve you from the tentacles of the thought's attempt to trap you.

How do you stop thinking about a certain thing? *Think about something else!* Good thought patterns must be entertained to displace evil ones. *"And the peace of God, which surpasses all understanding, shall keep your hearts and minds through Christ Jesus. Finally, brethren, whatsoever things are true, honest, just, pure, lovely, of good report; if there be any virtue, if there be any praise, think on these things. Those things, which*

93

you have both learned, and received, and heard, and seen in me, do: and the God of peace shall be with you." (Philippians 4:7-9).

- Pray and ask Abba, in the Name of Jesus, to help you **pull down this stronghold** and release you from its hold over you.

This is not a simple or a 'one-time-only' attempt. It has taken (*probably*) years to arrive at your present state so don't expect instant deliverance from it. It is usually a process of deliverance. "*For everyone who keeps on asking receives; and he who keeps on seeking finds; and to him who keeps on knocking, [the door] will be opened.*" (Matthew 7:8) "*Be well balanced (temperate, sober of mind), be vigilant and cautious at all times; for that enemy of yours, the devil, roams around like a lion roaring [in fierce hunger], seeking someone to seize upon and devour.*" (1Peter 5:8)

The Devil's Roar of Fear

There is an interesting story told of how lions hunt their prey. A group of lions is known as a 'pride.' They hunt as a well-disciplined unit. The superior male is usually the oldest and known for the ferocious voice exhibited in his roar. His voice (*roar*) has the ability to incite disabling fear in his intended victims. Unknown to these victims, the older lion is not as fleet of foot or as dangerous as he sounds. The true danger lies with the females and young males accompanying the elder male, not in the ferocity of his roar.

The pride stations their leader (the senior male) at the crest of an up-side-down "V." The legs of the "V" are made up of the rest of the pride ~ consisting of the females and younger males. Upon sighting an animal or group of animals to be selected as the meal for the day, all but the senior lion position themselves on either side of the unsuspecting victim(s), effectively surrounding him/them. The senior lion begins his mighty roaring while remaining stationary (or moving slightly forward). Simultaneously the two legs of the "V" begin to collapse toward the center. The victim(s), hearing the loud roaring and being extremely frightened, move away from the roar thinking to do so is to escape. In mistakenly moving away from the roar, the victim(s) rush headlong into the real danger (the rest of the pride) and are overtaken and devoured.

There is a parallel here in your fight with the devil. Scripture depicts the devil as a roaring lion seeking someone he may devour. The devil sounds a roar to distract you into running away from that which frightens you. This is exactly what he wants ~ to frighten you into running away from his roar into the trap he has set for you. The devil intends for the fear to control you so that you run away from it into his trap ~ your bondage to the fear.

A good rule of thumb to remember is, when you hear a roar from a person or a thing that scares you, move *toward* the sound rather than *away* from it. This will allow you to face and conquer your fears. It is better to confront and conquer your fear rather than flee from that which frightens you only to fall into a trap that is more damaging than the original fear.

An *imagined* fear is much greater than a *real* one!

Here is one of many examples. A person is guilty of fornication. The Holy Spirit is convicting him/her of the offense but the devil, as a counterfeit, roars the condemnation that to confess the sin will result in complete ruin for him/her. "Don't you dare admit you are guilty. People will think the very worst of you and will never accept you again."

This and other such nonsense is what I mean by 'the devil's roar of fear.' But by running *toward* the roar ~ facing and confessing the sin to God rather than running *away* from it (falling into the devil's trap) ~ the person can receive forgiveness of sin, renewal of the mind and become restored to God. If he/she runs away from the roar the devil wins and the person is trapped in anger, denial and condemnation.

Other weapons for our use are:

- <u>Knowledge of God's Word</u>. This cannot be stressed too strongly. The knowledge of exactly what the Scripture says and doesn't say regarding the current crisis you are facing is the key to effectively dealing with it. There must always be a balance between the letter of the Law and the Spirit of the Law. 1 Peter 5:8 gives you this important tenet that will assist in obtaining knowledge of Scripture. *"Be well balanced (temperate, sober of mind), be vigilant and cautious at all times..."* The Bible is filled with examples of being balanced when approaching decisions concerning certain subjects.

For example, when the woman who was caught in the very act of adultery was brought before Jesus, the Jewish law stated she was to be stoned to death. Jesus stated *"He of you who is without sin, cast the first stone."* And gave her mercy, setting aside the law. This is the scriptural balance of which I speak. Paul admonishes us in the wise use of scriptures by stating in 2 Corinthians 3:6 " ...*for the code [of the Law] kills, but the [Holy] Spirit makes alive.*" The Holy Spirit is the One who can direct your understanding of the scriptures into correct balance.

Study the Bible then ask the Holy Spirit to give you balance not compromise in its application.

- <u>Faith in God's authority and promises</u>. *"Without faith it is impossible to please God."* (Hebrews 11:6) *"For whatever does not originate and proceed from faith is sin [whatever is done without a conviction of its approval by God is sinful]."* (Romans 10:26) Faith is not a blind leap of "I wish." It is moving on the basis of what God has told me in His Word (review explanation of Faith in chapter 2).

- <u>The Name of Jesus</u>. Jesus told His disciples, *"And I will do [I Myself will grant] whatever you ask in My Name [as presenting all that I AM], so that the Father may be glorified and extolled in (through) the Son."* (John 14:13). The Name of Jesus is more powerful than any other name of any other person or any other item in existence. When, in the Name of Jesus, presenting all that Jesus is (I AM), you can be sure this is the most potent name you can use. The Name of Jesus must be used in faith in the power of His Name, trusting in no other. It is critical to *know what you mean* when you say, "In the Name of Jesus."

For example, in the book of Acts, some traveling Jewish exorcists (seven sons of a man named Sceva) attempted to use the Name of Jesus in this manner, *"I solemnly implore you and charge you by the Jesus Whom Paul preaches!"* This spirit replied, *"Jesus I know, and Paul I know about, but who are you?"* He then proceeded to beat them up, strip them of their clothing so that they dashed out of the house in fear, stripped naked and wounded. Evil spirits fear only persons who have a relationship with Jesus and who can use His name with knowledge and authority.

• The blood of Jesus. *"[The Father] has delivered and drawn us to Himself out of the control and dominion of darkness and has transferred us into the kingdom of the Son of His love, In Whom we have our redemption through His blood, [which means] the forgiveness of our sins."* (Colossians 1:13-14). *"For because of one man's trespass (lapse, offense) death reigned through that one, much more surely will those receive [God's] overflowing grace (unmerited favor) and the free gift of righteousness [putting them in right standing with Himself] reign as kings in life through the one man Jesus Christ (the Messiah, the Anointed One)."* (Romans 5:17)

These and many other scriptures announce the doom of Satan's message concerning your unworthiness, unrighteousness and guilt. Rejoice in your ability to use the Blood of Jesus with understanding of its protection from, and power to defeat all the schemes of the enemy.

• Your mouth. *"But the human tongue can be tamed by no man. It is a restless (undisciplined, irreconcilable) evil, full of deadly poison. With it we bless the Lord and Father, and with it we curse men who were made in God's likeness! Out of the same mouth come forth blessing and cursing. These things, my brethren, ought not to be so.* (James 3:8-10) *"For let him who wants to enjoy life and see good days [good — whether apparent or not] keep his tongue free from evil and his lips from guile (treachery, deceit).* (1 Peter 3:10) *"Death and life are in the power of the tongue, and they who indulge in it shall eat the fruit of it [for death or life]* (Proverbs 18:21) *"For where your treasure is, there will your heart be also."* (Matthew 6:21) Your priorities are very vital. Your treasure is where your heart is, and that's from whence the mouth speaks. *"For out of the fullness (the overflow, the superabundance) of the heart the mouth speaks.* (Matthew 12:34b)

Perhaps the mouth should be listed as a weapon both for and against man. I have chosen to list it as a very powerful weapon in its best use against the devil *"He who guards his mouth and his tongue keeps himself from troubles."* (Proverbs 21:23) Use your mouth and its tongue wisely.

- <u>Your ears</u>. *"He who has ears to hear, let him be listening and let him consider and perceive and comprehend by hearing."* (Matthew 11:15) *"So faith comes by hearing [what is told], and what is heard comes by the preaching [of the message that came from the lips] of Christ (the Messiah Himself)."* (Romans 10:17) With the correct use of your ears ~ hearing and listening ~ you can receive and move, with faith and understanding in the precepts of Jesus, effectively combating the enemy.

- <u>Your eyes</u>. *"Your eye is the lamp of your body; when your eye (your conscience) is sound and fulfilling its office, your whole body is full of light, but when it is not sound and is not fulfilling its office, your body is full of darkness. Be careful, therefore, that the light that is in you is not darkness.*" (Luke 11:34-35) This Scripture, spoken by Jesus, Himself refers to light as the revelation received through the eyes or conscience. We need to make correct choices regarding what revelation and information we will receive (from God or from the enemy). Godly revelation through the eyes of your conscience will result in a mighty weapon placed at your disposal for defeating the kingdom of darkness. It is important that you see *and* be observing with your eyes.

* <u>Knowledge of the character, ways and schemes of the devil.</u> Satan *never* wants to appear as Satan to you. He often appears as an angel of light (or something innocent), never as the father of lies or the essence of evil. For this reason, it is very important to be aware of his characteristics and profile, and his approach toward mankind. Anytime you find yourself in a situation that causes confusion instead of solutions, or that seems controlling, manipulative or condemning, you are facing influences that are characteristic of the devil. He thrives on deception and destruction, even to the extent of death. Satan is described as the father of lies; therefore, it should not be surprising to have him introduce these deceptive, negative, misleading and harmful characteristics into your life. These characteristics will occur in your relationships and situations, and are designed to mislead you into thinking anything but the truth about them.

These weapons are indeed mighty to the pulling down of strongholds and offer protection to the believer in his/her battles with the enemy of mankind. Only the use of these non-carnal weapons can defeat Satan and his kingdom of darkness. Become intimately acquainted with them and their use so you can become a warrior in this ongoing war.

Accurate information and understanding of Satan's personality and methods are among the most beneficial strategy that God will use to defeat him through Christ's Body. They are most effective in your storm-proof treatment for solving soul storms.

CHAPTER EIGHT

UNHOLY SOUL-TIES

The Breaking of Unholy Soul-Ties

The name "soul-tie" is taken from the scripture found in 1 Samuel 18 describing a wholesome relationship between David and King Saul's son, Jonathan. *"... the soul of Jonathan was knit with the soul of David, and Jonathan loved him as his own life.* (1Samuel 18:1).

As with many other things, Satan has chosen to pervert and counterfeit a wholesome soul-tie into an unholy alliance. It is this unholy partnership that will be addressed in this chapter. A few descriptive verses:

"But whoever commits adultery with a woman lacks heart and understanding (moral principle and prudence); he who does it is destroying his own life. Wounds and disgrace will he get, and his reproach will not be wiped away." (Proverbs 6:32-33)

"Beloved, I implore you as aliens and strangers and exiles [in this world] to abstain from sensual urges (the evil desires, the passions of the flesh, your lower nature) that wage war against the soul." (1Peter 2:11)

"So get rid of all uncleanness and the rampant outgrowth of wickedness, and receive and welcome the Word which implanted and rooted [in your hearts] contains the power to save your souls." (James 1:21)

The term 'soul-tie' refers to the binding of souls. When perverted, they become unholy soul-ties used by the devil to wither the quality of life through another of his 'blue northers' upon your life. This is another soul storm to be solved.

What are unholy soul-ties?

Unholy soul-ties are so called because of the bonding or tying of the soul with a person in an evil act of nature. Unholy soul-ties are part of the negative influence that lingers after the act, thought or influence is over or separated from you through forgiveness, or forgetfulness.

Unforgiveness is a good example of the negative results of an unholy soul-tie. Each time you see or think of the person that has hurt you, the grudge of unforgiveness gnaws away at you. If not removed, unholy soul-ties can cause bitterness, bondage and deep-seated torment. Unholy soul-ties are the counterfeit of healthy bonding such as spouse to spouse or parent to child and sibling relationships. They are perversions of healthy, righteous relationships and influences approved by God Himself.

Unholy soul-ties exist in mankind's two areas of body and soul. The free will of man directs his thoughts, actions and attitudes.

How do I break unholy soul-ties?

The breaking of unholy soul-ties and any associated curses is the same as any other act that pleases the Lord; it is done by faith in the Name of Jesus Christ.

PRAYER FOR BREAKING UNHOLY SOUL-TIES

Use a phrase similar to this, In Jesus' matchless Name, I break the unholy soul-tie with_____(*fill in the details*). [*I now ask the Holy Spirit if there are any curses attached to this soul-tie and if so advised, now speak the breaking of those curses, as well.*] I break the associated curse of_____(*name it and its details*), in Jesus' Name. I now declare myself free from the unholy soul-ties I have confessed before my Lord, as well as the associated curses, in the wonderful Name of Jesus Christ.

Amen!

How do unholy soul-ties start or begin?

All soul-ties have various origins: unholy body-unions and unholy soul-unions (in both the natural and supernatural realms). Therefore, let us explore some of these beginnings and causes of unholy soul-ties and their unions.

Unholy Body Unions

As you might suspect, unholy body-unions are concerned with the joining of your body to someone or something else in an unholy manner. This is can be either heterosexual or homosexual encounters. *"Or do you not know and realize that when a man joins himself to a prostitute, he becomes one body with her? The two, it is written, shall become one flesh [Genesis 2:24]. But the person who is united to the Lord becomes one spirit with Him. Shun all immorality and all sexual looseness [flee from impurity in thought, word, or deed]. Any other sin, which a man commits, is one outside the body, but he who commits sexual immorality sins against his own body. Do you not know that your body is the temple (the very sanctuary) of the Holy Spirit Who lives within you Whom you have received [as a gift] from God? You are not your own, you were bought with a price [purchased with a preciousness and paid for, made His own]. So then, honor God and bring glory to Him in your body."* (1Corinthians 6: 16-20)

There are several other scripture references pertaining to this area of unholy soul ties: Genesis 2:24, Matthew 19:5-9, and Ephesians 5:31-33. However, I feel the above reference from 1Corinthians is most descriptive.

Many, if not most of us, have sinned in the area of unholy body unions at one time or another in our lives. When the sin is over and you have been forgiven, there is still a lingering negative influence. This is known as an unholy soul-tie and should be broken to embrace the full freedom and peace of our Lord.

These offenses occur through fornication, adultery and perversion using the body. The remedy is to correctly recognize the offense and its participants (*who and what you did it with*), then confess it to God as sin and receive His forgiveness (*verbally if necessary*). You are now ready to break the unholy soul-tie with this offense. Repeat the above-suggested prayer for the breaking of Unholy Soul-Ties.

Several years ago, my wife and I had been ministering to a single woman who had been engaged in prostitution. We led her to salvation in Jesus Christ and helped her understand what repentance meant. But when we came to the area of breaking unholy soul-ties, she had a question. "I've had so many men I can't call their names in order to break this off me." We were instructed by God's Spirit impressing within us to tell her to recall the faces or any physical characteristic of the men to remind her of whom she was speaking, then merely say, "In Jesus' Name, I break the evil soul-tie with the person I am visualizing."

She was consequently free and delivered from the pain of her previous experiences. God also told us to tell her. "My daughter, I pronounce you free from sin and more clean and virtuous than you ever were as a virgin." That woman is now married to a wonderful man who is a believer and both are serving Jesus with their lives.

In another case, a friend of mine who was a minister of the Gospel had been delivered from addiction to homosexuality. Dave (*not his real name*) was ministering the breaking of unholy soul-ties in young men and women who were believers in Christ but caught up in homosexual relationships.

This particular day the minister Dave had two appointments, one in the morning and another in the afternoon. The morning appointment was with Danny (not his real name) and the breaking of the unholy soul-tie was with Danny's gay partner Josh (not his real name, either) at approximately 11:00AM.

Unknown to each other, Danny and Josh both wanted freedom from the addiction of this perverseness and each had made an appointment with Dave, the minister.

Josh came to his appointment in the afternoon and told Dave this story. "I knew God didn't want me involved in this kind of a relationship but its hold was too great on me. Even though I finally got the courage to make the appointment I was overcome with a reluctance to give up something I desired so much to the extent that I had made up my mind not to keep the appointment. At approximately 11:15AM ~ the exact time of Danny's deliverance ~ I had the strangest feeling come over me. I felt a stirring, a tearing and a ripping out from within my belly something so deep that I didn't know it was there. Afterwards, I felt only shame and remorse for what I had been doing and I knew that I must keep the appointment."

Dave then ministered the breaking of the unholy soul-tie between Josh and Danny. They repented, confessed their sins and are now individually restored and set free to serve the Lord Jesus Christ.

Unholy Soulish Unions

Not only are there sins made with the **body** creating unholy soul-ties, there are sins committed with the **soul** (mind, will and emotions). Unholy *mental* or *emotional* relationships also cause unholy soul-ties. These types of relationships can be within <u>family members and relatives</u>. Abuse and neglect, rejection and abandonment are but some of the ways these unholy soul-ties are created.

Other areas of unholy soul-tie origins are within <u>friendships, gangs or cultic membership</u>. Included in these are *verbal* oaths, vows and covenants spoken in front of others or while alone.

Note: *One such experience in my life was the vows and oaths I spoke and swore to when becoming a member of a Masonic organization.*

Other doorways for unholy soul-ties' entrance are contracts and promises made either *written or verbal* that contain dark-side commitments. This includes cheating, defrauding or willful defaulting of these contracts and promises on your behalf or on the part of another. Sometimes friendships are sources of soulish involvement. The kind of friendship that has deteriorated into manipulation, control or seduction can become a soul-tie that is debilitating.

When I was in the sixth or seventh grade, I had a friend named Joe. He and I went to all the movies available (usually on Saturdays). Several of the movies depicted 'blood brothers' in which two young men cut their palms so that their blood flowed. They made vows to remain true 'blood brothers' and clasped their hands together so the blood would mingle. My friend Joe and I thought that was really cool (we didn't call it 'cool' in those days) so we did the same thing. We cut our palms, let the blood mingle and said we would be 'blood brothers' forever. A year or so later I moved away and we never saw each other again.

I didn't become a 'sold-out' believer in Christ until I was in my mid-forties so it had to be some thirty to thirty-five years later that the Lord reminded me of the vows Joe and I made creating an unholy soul-tie that needed to be broken.

God did not explain to me why it was evil or unholy. I have not seen Joe or heard from him since then and knew absolutely nothing about his physical, soulish or spiritual health, I only knew I must obey what God said to do and break off those vows and the soul tie.

Authority figures are another potential for bondage of the soul. Persons such as parents, relatives, siblings, teachers, supervisors, pastors, etc. with unholy, destructive purposes, words or actions are likely roots of unholy soul-ties.

These persons will be those who perverted the wholesome intentions and actions of godly relationships resulting in bondage from which you need deliverance.

Numbers, chapter 30, states that a man who vows, gives an oath or makes a pledge is not to break or profane his word. *"He shall do according to all that proceeds out of his mouth."* You can immediately see that it is most important to guard what comes out of the mouth because you are to do all that proceeds out of your mouth. This also helps explain how you give the devil legal rights to molest and manipulate through *"all that proceeds out of your mouth."* The same chapter gives some important instructions concerning women.

If a woman vows a vow to the Lord and binds herself by a pledge while in her father's house in her youth, and her father hears her vow and offers no objection, then her vows stand. But if her father refuses to allow her [to carry out her vows] on the day that he hears about it, not any of her vows or her pledges with which she has bound herself shall stand. And the Lord will forgive her because her father refused to let her [carry out her purpose].

The passage in Numbers 30 proceeds on to say, that if she is married and her husband says nothing, the vow stands. But if after hearing her vow he disallows or annuls it, the vow is annulled and the Lord will forgive her. Likewise, a single, widow or a divorced woman's vows will stand against her.

This agrees with the passage in 1Corinthians 11, *"But I want you to know and realize that Christ is the Head of every man, and the head of a woman is her husband, and the Head of Christ is God."* Verse 11 states, *"Nevertheless in [the plan of] the Lord and from His point of view woman is not apart from and independent of man, nor is man aloof from and independent of woman."* (1Corinthians 11:3-11)

I think this proposes that only from your authority (the one to whom you should submit) do you receive annulment of your vows. When you are in authority over someone (children, etc.), it is therefore your responsibility to guard the communication that comes out of his or her mouth, judging whether to allow it to stand or not. Many 'blue northers' occur because those who refuse to take their responsibilities seriously, do not carry out this guarding of the words of the mouth.

"But if the watchman sees the sword coming and does not blow the trumpet and the people are not warned, and the sword comes and takes away any one of them; he is taken away in and for his perversity and iniquity, but his blood will I require at the watchman's hand." (Ezekiel 33:6)

This admonition to be a watchman over those who are our responsibility (family, business, etc.) includes guarding the words that come from the mouth as well as providing for them.

Unholy Spiritual or Supernatural Unions

You have seen how unholy soul-ties can be initiated through sins made in the body and sins made through the soul. Let's now look at how you can commit sins through the supernatural realm resulting in unholy soul-ties.

"There shall not be found among you anyone who makes his son or daughter pass through the fire, or who uses divination, or is a soothsayer, or an augur, or a sorcerer, or a charmer, or a medium, or a wizard, or a necromancer." (Deuteronomy 18:10-11)

God is very specific with His commandments of some things in which He does not want His people participating.

In Deuteronomy, chapters 27 and 28, God has all the people (Israel) to gather on two mountains, Mount Gerizim to bless the people and Mount Ebal to pronounce a curse for disobedience.

I will only address the curse issue. Included was anyone who made a graven image, one who dishonored his parents, removed a neighbor's landmark, mislead a blind (disabled) man, perverted justice, adultery, bestiality, incest, murder, bribery and anyone who did not support and agree with the words of the law being passed down.

God listed in great detail the nature of the curses that will not only follow, but will overtake you when you commit any of the above offenses. He concluded with this verse: *"All these curses shall come upon you and shall pursue you and overtake you till you are destroyed, because you do not obey the voice of the Lord your God, to keep His commandments and His statutes which He commanded you."* (Deuteronomy 28:45)

God only commands things that are beneficial for you; therefore, the things He forbids are *not* good for you. Committing things forbidden by God opens doorways of entrance through which Satan and his demons can legally enter and conduct destruction. This will indeed bring a 'blue norther' into your life.

When a person involves himself or herself in the supernatural area without the protection of the Holy Spirit, he or she finds opportunity for involvement in unholy practices forbidden by God. Consequently, doorways saying, *"Come in"* are opened for Satan and his bunch in your life.

Dabbling in the areas of witches, warlocks, mediums, covens, the occult or cult relationships and/or their paraphernalia, astrology, horoscope, divination, water-witching or other psychic forces' activity and idolatry are forbidden areas in which God does not want his children participating. This also includes some of the video and Internet games now being sold as entertainment.

If you find that you have entered into or been involved in any of these areas or if dependent children of yours have been involved, you (or your children) have an unholy soul-tie to it that needs to be broken and renounced.

To summarize, the soul storms of unholy soul-ties occur through unholy *body* unions, unholy *soulish* unions, and unions with unholy spiritual or supernatural *forces and practices.*

Just remember how to recognize the attacks and break the effects and influences of unholy soul-ties. This is one more way in which you are able to become truly storm-proof in the midst of your soul storms.

CHAPTER NINE

THE BREAKING OF CURSES

The definition of <u>curse</u>: To utter a wish of evil against one; to injure; to subject to evil; to vex, harass or torment with great calamities; to devote to evil.

Curses occur in the lives of people today. Have you ever wondered why certain things keep happening to a family for several generations? Why are certain traits in one generation mirrored in succeeding generations? Why do these same storms keep recurring in my family?

Why are you just like your father, grandfather, etc.?

A certain grandfather was a rough-mannered individual who physically and verbally abused his wife and children. He had several extramarital adulterous affairs, drank too much, gambled excessively and showed little if any affection to his children. Several addictive habits dominated his life and he had many health problems, dying of a heart attack in his sixties.

His children, especially males, grew up to be almost exactly like him. They found women who seemed to cry out for male abuse and physical dominance. They abused their wives and children; they drank, slept around, did drugs, gambled and indulged themselves in much the same way their father (the grandfather) did with poor health as a consequence.

Due to this state of health the children of this grandfather also begin to die off as they reached their sixties.

Children born to these second-generation families found themselves following the same degenerating patterns of existence as their father and grandfather. (*I am just like my father who was just like his father*). The spiral of death gets deeper and steeper.

The pattern this family suffers from is one of a curse or curses being passed down to its successors. You can probably recall some friends and families with similar symptoms and results. This destructive pattern must be broken, so that health and wholesomeness can be restored.

What causes curses in the first place?

A curse has a reason for happening, and sin in one form or another is the reason. Proverbs 26:2 states, *"As the sparrow in her wandering, as the swallow in her flying, so the causeless curse does not alight."* In Genesis 3:14-19, God curses the serpent, Eve, Adam and the whole earth because of Adam's sin.

All that God cursed is dying. Only through accepting and believing Jesus Christ on a personal basis can you be delivered from this curse. This decision is from a spiritual dimension that manifests itself in the natural. If you function in the natural or supernatural realms without Jesus Christ in your life, you are subject to natural law and therefore under the curse (Galatians 4:4,5). We must walk according to the Spirit. (Galations 5:16-18)

What are the laws of curses?

• <u>Things devoted to God</u> create curses if used in other ways or for other purposes. (Leviticus 27:28b, Malachi 3:8-9)

• A curse can only enter through <u>doorways left open to it.</u> (Deuteronomy 27:15-26, 28:15-45)

• A curse is removed permanently only <u>after the sin is removed.</u> (Galatians 3:10-13)

• The <u>power of the curse is demonic.</u> (Genesis 3:15, Ephesians 4:26-27)

• The good news in all this is, <u>Jesus bore the penalty for the curse.</u> (Galations 3:13-14)

Where do curses come from or start?

Curses begin in various ways. These include spoken words, breaking of promises, occult or cultic involvement, heritage from ancestors, and misusing things dedicated to God. I will develop these topics concerning the origins of curses in detail as we go along.

<u>Spoken Words</u>

Curses have a variety of beginnings. Some are known and recognized, others are not. One of these beginnings is the spoken word. These are words spoken by *others* that affect you.

1) <u>Words in statements</u> such as "You are no good, you will amount to nothing, you are useless, you can never

catch on to that, etc." can bring curses in your life. Phrases similar to these that are spoken by relatives, friends, authority figures (including parents, siblings, nannies, sitters, schoolmates, teachers, bosses, pastors and the like) can be the cause of much anguish.

When persons you are influenced by speak negative words and you find yourself in *agreement* with what is said by them (because of their authority and influence), then a curse can be set in motion.

2) Words spoken in vengeance or anger toward you from virtually *anyone* concerning *any subject* from a schoolyard argument to cutting someone off in traffic can become the origin of a curse. Again, you must *not* agree with these statements when you hear them. Remember *"the causeless curse will not alight."*

3) Words of negative "self-talk" about yourself, *to* yourself, *by* yourself which can also cause a curse to begin. Examples of negative *"self-talk"* are: "I never can do anything right." "I am a failure and have been all my life." "I can never do anything about my temper (or addiction)." "I will never be accepted by that person, group, or school." "I can't do that, etc." "Why even try?"

This "self-talk" can also be spoken aloud to others *about yourself* in an effort to appear humble. "Self-talk" of this type is just as destructive as are those words spoken of you by others. If you are engaged in this type of destructive "self-talk,' stop it and replace it with uplifting, positive words.

Words *causing* curses can be directed toward you at *any* time. Only when you <u>agree</u> with what is said or implied, and by <u>allowing sin</u> in some form to <u>remain</u> in your life after the words are spoken, will you let the power of a curse *begin and/or continue*.

<u>Broken Promises</u> (written or spoken)

Another beginning for curses is the breaking of oaths, vows, contracts, covenants or *written* pacts. These verbal or written acknowledgements become promises that bind one person to another person or group of persons.

Perhaps the most recognizable example of this kind is *divorce*. By definition, divorce is the breaking apart or putting asunder a union made with sacred vows before God. This is not meant to put divorced persons under condemnation, however, it is necessary to realize that you have broken vows made before God.

Many times there is a breaking of the vows made before God *without* a legal divorce. There can be covert (secret) infidelity such as pornography, lustful thoughts, unholy fantasies and yearnings. There can also be overt (open) actions such as adultery, flirting and homosexuality. In all cases, confess it as sin, repent and accept God's forgiveness, seek His direction for your life and proceed from there. (*To do less is to invite a curse into your life*).

Other binding vows are those of a *written* contract. If you are the cause of a contract or covenant being broken, confess it as sin before God, receive His forgiveness, ask

His direction for your life (*including restitution*) and proceed.

If another person is responsible for the breaking of the written covenant, exercise forgiveness (*explained in chapter 3*) for the offense, receive God's promise of release, then walk in peace.

Cultic or occult involvement

Some beginnings of curses occur through cultic or occult involvement. The term cult as it is used here, is defined as a system of religious worship that does not include Jesus as the Christ. A cult also includes devoted attachment (*worship)* of/to a person or principle. David Koresh and his branch Davidians, as well as Jim Jones and his followers, are well-known recent examples.

The occult, on the other hand, is defined as the study of evil ~ especially Satanism. Tarot cards and their reading, Ouija boards, astrology, video and Internet games with demonic content, witchcraft, hexes and spells are some of the occult devices.

The beginnings of curses from cultic and occult involvement occur for two reasons.

1) The cultic and occult exposure involves the supernatural realm. As stated earlier, without an acceptance of Jesus the Christ as Savior, the supernatural realm and its power is beyond the ability of natural man to successfully withstand the onslaught of Satan, thereby allowing a curse to begin and continue.

2) Worship of any god but Yahweh is to violate the first of the Ten Commandments, also resulting in a curse. When a person has been involved in either a cult or the occult, then afterward becomes a believer, you can simply break the power of the curses associated with your former involvement in the Name and power of Jesus Christ.

There may be spoken curses placed upon you by others involved in the occult or a cult after you have severed relationship with them as well. These curses can also be broken and/or prevented. This is to follow the confession of your sin, embracing repentance and renunciation, and accepting the forgiveness of God through Jesus Christ. You then protect your life by applying the blood of Jesus as an aid in the prevention of curses.

There may also exist the need to break the unholy soul-ties with the members and purposes of the organization(s). (See explanation of breaking unholy soul-ties in Chapter 8).

Ancestral Heritage

Still another beginning for curses is the heritage from ancestors based on race or culture. For example, if your ancestors were from a pagan culture that worshipped foreign gods, the curse on that practice may need to be broken from you in Jesus' Name.

An example would be, children born to known Nazi parents that might have curses following them of an anti-Semite (*hatred of the Jews*) nature, as well as the curse of embracing a super-race mentality. Buddhism, Islam, Ku Klux Klan and etc. involvement by ancestors can have curses associated with it that are passed down into a person's life as well.

Each national origin or ethnic group has ancestral practices that are evil or unholy in nature and subsequently provide avenues from which curses are passed along to descendents. Evil and unholy actions of ancestral or inherited sources are to be identified; you can then begin the process of breaking the associated curses.

Misuse of Devoted Things

An area where we as Christians are probably the most ignorant and the most disobedient is the misuse of devoted things. There are certain things that are devoted exclusively to God. Among these things is the tithe (ten-percent). *"Will a man rob or defraud God? Yet you rob and defraud Me. But you say, In what way do we rob or defraud You? [You have withheld your] tithes and offerings. You are cursed with a curse, for you are robbing Me, even this whole nation."* (Malachi 3:8-9)

If the tithe is not given to the Lord, a curse follows. Many times this takes the form of a curse of poverty. God's mathematics declares you can get by better financially with only ninety percent (*giving God His tithe*) than you can with one hundred-percent (*not giving God His tithe*).

Sowing and reaping is the central theme in the Kingdom of God. Therefore, if there is no sowing (*God's tithe*); there will be no reaping (*your harvest*). The tithe is the devoted thing and is God's alone. It needs to be given first.

When the devoted thing is given, God is then obliged to bless the remainder. If God has nothing to work with (*His tithe*), He has nothing with which to bless you. If the tithe is given last rather than first, the ninety-percent cannot be blessed because the tithe is what redeems and sanctifies the one hundred-percent. This is the first step toward financial success with the Lord. There are either blessings or curses. This includes your finances. The tithe is on the gross.

Another of God's devoted things is the "first mentioned" or "first of everything:" the first fruits, the first born, etc. If the first is not given to God it is cursed.

Initiate a spiritual inventory of your life. See if there are devoted things that you are in the process of withholding. Ask God to forgive you and begin rectifying the wrong immediately. Break the curses associated with this and live in victory in Christ.

To summarize the origins of curses:

1.   The spoken word (from others or from myself).
2.   The breaking of oaths, vows, promises or contracts (either verbal or written).
3.   Involvement in cults or the occult.
4.   Heritage from ancestors.
5.   Misuse of things devoted to God.

These are ways curses can and do enter our lives.

How do I get rid of or break curses?

To break a curse, as has been stated above, consists of walking through the following steps:

- Identify the specific nature of the curse (*using suggestions from above*).

- Speak aloud to the specific curse and its cause.

- Use the power vested in the Name of Jesus (*in faith*).

- Cast out any accompanying evil or unholy spirits in the Name of Jesus.

- Receive (*in faith*) the freedom from the bondage of the curse.

- Call on the Holy Spirit to fill the vessel (*the person under the curse*) with the opposite influence (*by name*) of what was cast out.

- Close any sin doors associated with the curse (*activities, objects, thoughts, words, etc.*). This may involve crucifixion of the flesh, confession of sin or casting out satanic influences or any combination.

- Thank and praise God for His deliverance.

A sample prayer follows.

PRAYER FOR THE BREAKING OF CURSES

Father, I recognize You as the supreme authority over all things. I hereby submit my life to You. In the Name of Jesus, I break the curse of _____ *(identify with as much detail as possible)* _upon my life. I confess the associated sin(s) of_ *(be very specific)* and repent and renounce my involvement in this. By Your Word, I will make restitution.

I now receive Your forgiveness, thereby declaring myself free from the bondage and influence of the curse. I glorify You for Your grace and mercy and the power to break this awful thing off me, in Jesus' matchless Name. Amen!

Through discovering and solving the soul storms of curses mentioned above, the believer in Christ can successfully withstand them. Thereby, becoming storm-proof when their destructiveness occurs.

CHAPTER TEN

BLOODLINES & ANCESTRAL/ENVIRONMENTAL INIQUITIES

What is the difference in iniquities and bloodlines?

Iniquity by definition: The sins or the tendency, propensity and influence towards sin passed down through the sin(s) of the fathers. Iniquity is further defined as perversity or depravity – guilt, contracted by sinning – anything unjustly acquired; the absence of equity or improper balance.

Bloodlines by definition: A person's inherited personality traits contained in the blood type and its genetic makeup. Pedigree is a synonym and applies to the bloodline or lineage. Scripture declares the life is in the blood; it is reasonable to believe that the negative influence governing the tendency to sin and weakness lie within the bloodlines of ancestors passed down to descendents.

"As for the life of all flesh, the blood of it represents the life of it;" (Leviticus 17:14)

Ancestral iniquities and bloodlines are similar to some curses in that they are inherited or obtained from someone or somewhere else outside the person. Sometimes the environment is the sole evil influence. At other times it is the ancestral bloodline.

Environment by definition: The surroundings or the conditions surrounding that affect the development of someone.

There is also the combination of all three: bloodlines, ancestral, and environmental iniquities. This is not to be feared but recognized as a source of supernatural influence through which the kingdom of darkness can attack and vex.

An alcoholic father passes the propensity to alcohol craving to his children. A woman who shoplifts passes the desire to steal to her children. A mother, nanny or sitter whose anger at less than perfection in keeping a room clean, exerts unhealthy boundary lines, influencing her children to bouts of anger and rage when things are not orderly. These are but a few examples of how iniquities and bloodlines can be passed along to other persons, children, and children's children.

Environmental, ethnic and cultural issues are contributors to iniquities and the subsequent passing of them along to heirs. These are called environmental iniquities.

Ancestral iniquities however, are confined to blood relationships (*as are bloodlines*) and are not passed along to non-blood-connected individuals. *"... For I the Lord your God am a jealous God, visiting the iniquity of the fathers upon the children to the third and fourth generation of those who hate Me. But showing mercy and steadfast love to a thousand generations to those who love Me and keep My commandments."* (Exodus 20:5-6)

"Woe to those who draw [calamity] with cords of iniquity and falsehood, who bring punishment to themselves with a cart rope of wickedness, Who say, Let [the holy One] make haste and speed His [prophesied] vengeance, that we may see it; and let the purpose of the Holy One of Israel draw near and come, that we may know it! Woe to those who call evil good and good evil, who put darkness for light and light for darkness, who put bitter for sweet and sweet for bitter! Woe to those who are wise in their own eyes and prudent and shrewd in their own sight! Woe to those who are mighty heroes at drinking wine and men of strength in mixing alcoholic drinks! — Who justify and acquit the guilty for a bribe, but take away the rights of the innocent and righteous from them! Therefore, as the tongue of fire devours the stubble, and as the dry grass sinks down in the flame, so their root shall be like rottenness and their blossom shall go up like fine dust — because they have rejected and cast away the law and the teaching of the Lord of hosts and have not believed but have treated scornfully and have despised the word of the Holy One of Israel." (Isaiah 5:18-24)

The familiar spirit operating through a person's tendencies toward certain weaknesses, addictions and cravings aids the developing and passing down of iniquities through bloodlines and environment. I will discuss the familiar spirit in more detail later.

Drives of Iniquity

There are some hidden principles of rebellion against constituted authority, which are called the Drives of Iniquity. These can occur from *personal* iniquity, *environmental* iniquity, *bloodline* iniquity or from a combination of all three. Notice the strong emphasis on 'self' and its aggrandizement.

- <u>Self-righteousness</u> – approval based upon your own performance and quality. The standard is yourself and you'll measure everything and everyone by that yardstick.

- <u>Self-exaltation</u> – a desire to be above others with promotion of yourself. It is pride, to the extent you think more highly of yourself than others, and less highly of others than you do yourself.

- <u>Self-appointment</u> – seeking to belong by self-aggrandizement. It is taking an authoritative position or promotion belonging to another rather than being promoted especially from God.

- <u>Self-display</u> – seeking recognition or approval for egotistical or personal desires and satisfaction.

- <u>Self-sustaining</u> – I, me, mine, ours, as the most important person(s) in any comparison. Depending upon yourself for the answers and the source of your own existence.

These principles are very close to the surface in many of us and contribute to the iniquities we are committing and passing on to our heirs. As you can see there are several sources of iniquities and how they affect behavior.

"My people perish for lack of knowledge." (Hosea 4:6)

This familiar passage suggests 'a lack of knowledge' is one of the main reasons Satan is able to defeat you and me. It is time for understanding, examination and elimination of these iniquities in order to become fashioned into the image of Jesus thereby "storm-proofing" your life.

When diagnosing and casting out personal and/or environmental iniquities, and bloodlines, the associated demons are to be named and cast out as well.

Environmental influences from family, culture or race are also to be considered and dealt with accordingly (sometimes it is necessary to break unholy soul-ties, curses, unforgiveness, etc.).

This bondage of iniquity through bloodlines and environment are other soul storms or 'blue northers' blown in by the enemy of man to cripple and prevent the abundant life promised by Jesus. Fortunately, they can be broken in the same manner as curses are broken (described in chapter 9) ~ by receiving and using the power and authority found in the Name of Jesus. Becoming free from the entangling tendrils of bondage passed down by ancestors and /or environment will allow you to become truly storm-proof in your walk with the Lord.

CHAPTER ELEVEN

DEMONIZATION — ROOTS & FRUIT

One of the fiercest of soul storms faced by believers is that of demonization. God's love is never failing and also provides a way for man to withstand even this fierce storm. All of God's remedies for man's problems (*after salvation*) are similar. When needed, they must be practiced continually, habitually and by faith in the Name of Jesus. This is certainly true as it pertains to demonization.

By demonization I mean the deliberate effort from the demonic kingdom to influence, harass, vex, torment or otherwise control a human subject. This can be very subtle at times, manifesting itself either in a covert or overt manner.

Satan attacks through **sin doors** opened to him. These doorways include sin in various forms such as 1) willful disobedience [*in actions, thoughts and words*]; 2) ignorance of Satan and his methods; 3) inherited traits, weaknesses and addictions; 4) iniquities both inherited and environmental.

Let me make one thing very apparent at the onset. When a person has been born again by asking and receiving the Lord Jesus Christ into his or her life, there can be *no possession* of that believer's spirit by demons. There can certainly be oppression and influence by demons, but not possession. The Holy Spirit possesses the born-again human spirit and there is no room for a demon.

The phrase, "A Christian can't have a demon." is true unless the Christian wants and invites a demon by leaving a door open for one. The demonization to which I am referring is in the *soulish* and *body* areas of man, not his *spirit*.

Demonization, not unlike physical illnesses can have deceptive symptoms. If only the symptoms are treated, the true cause of the malady is left untreated and is free to re-occur. For this reason, it is important to discern the "root" cause of the problem, bind and cast it out. Failure to focus on the source of disability is to become occupied with ejecting only the "fruit" of the "root." This inevitably leaves the recurrence of the "fruit," since the "root" is not destroyed. The "fruit" may resemble its "root," but in order to become totally free from bondage, the removal of the "root" is critical to eliminate regrowth of "fruit."

"I am the Vine; you are the branches. Whoever lives in Me and I in him bears much (abundant) fruit. However, apart from Me [cut off from vital union with Me] you can do nothing." (John 15:5)

This passage illustrates two points: First, the relationship between fruit and its root, and God's primary purpose and example of fruitful living.

"But the fruit of the [Holy] Spirit [the work which His Presence within accomplishes] is love, joy (gladness), peace, patience (an even temper, forbearance), kindness, goodness (benevolence), faithfulness, Gentleness (meekness, humility), self-control (self-restraint, continence). Against such things there is no law [that can bring a charge]." (Galatians 5:22-23)

It is important to see that demonization is an exact counterfeit of the root and fruit spoken of by Jesus. Jesus is the vine, we are the branches (John 15:5 above). Connected to Jesus, we produce the fruit of the Spirit. Satan, counterfeiting this concept, sets himself up as the source of evil. His demon roots are the opposite influences from the fruit of the Spirit and produce evil fruit in a person's life. Demonic fruit, just as Spiritual fruit, cannot live without attachment to its root.

This chapter will help those of you who suffer from lingering evil or unholy influences to ascertain whether the influence is a "root" spirit or one of its "fruit." Evil influences continue because the 'root' spirit was not effectively dealt with and allowed more evil 'fruit' to reproduce.

The chapter can also help those preparing for this area of ministry.

Discerning of Spirits

It is very important to listen to the Holy Spirit and discern what spirits are being dealt with *before* taking any action.

"Beloved, do not put faith in every spirit, but prove (test) the spirits to discover whether they proceed from God; for many false prophets have gone forth into the world. By this you may know (perceive and recognize) the Spirit of God: every spirit which acknowledges and confesses [the fact] that Jesus Christ (the Messiah) [actually] has become man and has come in the flesh is of God [has God for its source]; and every spirit which does not acknowledge and confess that Jesus Christ has come in

the flesh [but would annul, destroy, sever, disunite Him] is not of God [does not proceed from Him]. This [non-confession] is the [spirit] of the antichrist, [of] which you heard it was coming, and now it is already in the world. Little children, you are of God [you belong to Him] and have [already] defeated and overcome them [the agents of the antichrist], because He Who lives in you is greater (mightier) than he who is in the world." (1 John 4:1-4)

As a believer, you are to discern the difference in spirits and whether they proceed from God. The above passage explains how. Discernment is also a *gift of the Spirit* given when you are baptized in the fullness of the Holy Spirit and is described thusly, *"To another the ability to discern and distinguish between [the utterances of true] spirits [and false ones]...All these [gifts, achievements, abilities] are inspired and brought to pass by one and the same [Holy] Spirit, Who apportions to each person [exactly] as He chooses."* (1Corinthians 12:10b, 11b)

As you can see, God expects you to learn to discern the supernatural forces with which you come in contact. Discerning between evil spirits and the Spirit of God consists of listening to the message of the spirit.

To confuse the issue, Satan attempts to influence your mind and its selfish desires to think his thoughts in situations you face. The language of the mind is your thoughts, fantasies and imaginations. Again, ask yourself what is the theme of the message you are receiving?

In ministry situations (especially demonization) the voices are strong and varied. Satan is very clever. Whether by inflicting pain and suffering through having people *underestimate* his power, or by deceiving people to *overestimate* his power, he can work believers into exhaustion by attempting to cast demons out of every suspicious person and situation (a demon behind every bush).

God showed my wife and me that as we developed certain spiritual skills, we would be practicing in the exact area where we were learning and growing. In our case at the time, it was in areas of discernment, demonization and casting out evil spirits. We knew that if a person had a demon, the power of faith in the Name and Blood of the Lord Jesus Christ was sufficient to cast it out. The greatest problem came in the area of discernment.

For practice, we would go into high traffic places like the Mall or restaurants and 'let our spirits open up' to what we could discern. There was a mixture of our imagination, observation, and spiritual discernment working as we practiced and learned to fine-tune our gift of "discerning of spirits." I can imagine our Abba smiling down on His two children who became brave enough to receive, and learn and practice a gift He had bestowed upon them. I am sure it delighted Him when we succeeded and amused Him as we discovered and corrected our errors.

Slowly we began to differentiate between the flesh and its voice and clearly started to recognize evil and its manifestations. Amazingly, the voice of God through His Holy Spirit became more and more apparent as we sought Him.

Equally amazing was that the more we sought the voice of the Lord, the less we had to rely on discerning the voice of evil. Jesus said *"The sheep that are My own hear and are listening to My voice; and I know them, and they follow Me."* (John 10:27) It no longer became so important to know the name or function of evil spirits, but only recognize there was something that needed expulsion.

When you are in ministry situations, where do these strange emotional feelings come from?

One more warning concerning the discerning of spirits. When your sensitivity increases in the identification of what spirit is present in an individual who is under the influence of demonic activity, there is the possibility of 'picking up' or transferring that influence to your own life. Let me illustrate.

My wife is extremely sensitive to the workings of evil spirits in and around individuals and/or locations. Several times, after completing ministry situations, we would come away from the session with depression, anger, lust, perversion, hopelessness and even suicidal thoughts. These were much more prevalent in Joyce than they were in me. But in both cases (hers or mine) we were unable to distinguish the difference in these "new" emotions from those of our very own.

We discovered this one time through a statement I made to Joyce, "That's not like you to be feeling like that." Immediately the Holy Spirit said, "Yes, that's right. The feeling is not yours or hers." From that moment on, when a strange emotion or stray thought came through us, we refused to agree with or entertain its negative influences and feelings being thrust upon us ~ another avenue to freedom within soul storms.

For those of you with deep feelings of compassion, helping and/or mercy, become aware that the enemy can cause you to experience *precisely the same* emotions and thoughts of someone around you. He frequently exploits the natural motivations within you and presents counterfeit emotions and desires that will sidetrack you from the real issues God wants you to face. This may define some of the unexplained moods to which you are exposed and fall prey to, rather than blaming them on physical or natural causes.

As stated earlier, the difference between God's remedies is not unlike the differences in medical remedies. Some are administered from a hygienic, remedial or maintenance standpoint; others are from a therapeutic or restorative basis.

You can easily determine the difference between the "root" and its "fruit" through superior discernment provided by the Holy Spirit to you. Listed are the unholy root spirit, its counterpart in God's kingdom, a brief description of associated fruit (*manifested with its presence*) and a Scripture reference where possible.

The demonic manifestations in each area listed are the goals and objectives each demon is striving to obtain!

"But if I cast out devils by the Spirit of God, Then the Kingdom of God is come unto you. Or else how can one enter into a strong man's house and spoil his goods, except he first bind the strong man? And then he will spoil his house." (Matthew 12:28-29)

FAMILIAR SPIRIT –vs.- HOLY SPIRIT

The familiar spirit is sometimes translated medium or wizard.

> (Leviticus 19: 31; 20:6, 27; Deuteronomy 18:11; 1Samuel 28: 3, 7-9; 2 Kings 21:6; 23:24; 1Chronicles 10:13; 2 Chronicles 33:6; Isaiah 8:19; 19:3; 29:4)

Familiar spirits are spoken of specifically by name in the Bible. They are strong major spirits whose assignment it is to know you, influence you in a negative or evil way then lead you into error. *"Turn not to those [mediums] who have familiar spirits or to wizards; do not seek them out to be defiled by them. I am the Lord your God."* (Leviticus 19:31)

The *familiar spirit* has three directives to follow in its commission:

Directive one: To know you, your habits, preferences, pleasures, likes, dislikes, favorites, weakness to temptation, susceptibility to disease and illness.

Directive two: Use the familiar information gained to influence you negatively into or towards evil. To control you to the degree you have nothing to do with God and His purposes. The key word is 'control.'

Directive three: By communicating with *familiar spirits* in other persons, exchange this information to lead you and others into error. The end objective is to disrupt the purposes of God in your life, rendering you defeated and powerless while you submit to and serve evil purposes.

Notice that the *familiar spirit* is Satan's imitation of the Holy Spirit. The Holy Spirit (*Greek: parakletos meaning one called alongside as intercessor, consoler, advocate, and comforter*) is to guide, reprove, convict, instruct and accompany with divine power in all aspects of life.

The Holy Spirit is intimately acquainted with you. He knows your 'highs' and your 'lows.' He knows your weaknesses to temptations and your tendencies toward good and evil. He knows where you are compassionate and where you are indifferent. The Holy Spirit knows how your environment has influenced you and what your inherited ancestral traits are. The Holy Spirit understands personality types that 'set you off.' He also knows the difference in your 'wants' and your 'needs.' He provides answers to all your problems by exerting the power of God's grace and provisions of His mercy (*which are new every morning.* (Lamentations 3:22b)

The enemy of man counterfeits this spiritual influence of the Holy Spirit substituting instead a *familiar spirit* to assist and control you in misbehavior, sin, condemnation and false instruction.

Satan's counterfeit is called alongside as an accuser; the one who condemns, confuses, divides and disturbs your relationships of all kinds (*especially marriages and family unions*). Its power comes through detailed knowledge of your ancestral weakness, iniquity, your proclivity to sin, as well as your negative personality quirks.

The *familiar spirit* is imitating the Holy Spirit's purpose of convicting you of sin, righteousness and judgement (John 16:8) through condemnation, judgement and temptation. The counterfeit attempts to guide you and influence you by deception and manipulation. He attempts to condemn you and accuse your judgements (and misjudgments) in successful relationships. He accompanies you while exerting evil influences to defeat you in all areas of your life.

This spirit can be passed down to you from various family members. It has the ability to become very intimate in knowledge of a family or individual. It becomes so familiar with your tendencies and choices it sometimes seems that the familiar spirit can read your mind. However, it cannot. But we betray our innermost thoughts by our habits and ill-advised mutterings to the extent it knows you very well. You whose ancestors (*or perhaps you yourself*) have been involved in spiritualism and the occult have opened doors to the *familiar spirit's* entrance and exploitation.

Another manifestation of the *familiar spirit* occurs in the perpetuation of curses (*alcoholism, suicide, depression, addictions, divorce, etc.*) known to a family or individual. It not only assists the curses' persistence in a family or individual, but also promotes open doors to curses through related sins and weaknesses as well.

A further conspicuous piece of evidence of the familiar spirit is the voice of condemnation concerning your past sins, an abuse of your tendency and propensity toward sin, and the enhancing of your unholy personal traits of ancestry. Statements (from yourself or others) such as "That's just the way you are, you'll never change."

"You know you want to do it so just go ahead." "If nobody gets hurt it's okay to do it." "God will never forgive you of that sin." All of which heaps layer on layer of bondage in your life.

Become aware that demonic forces are listening and writing down everything negative that comes from your speech. Guard carefully what comes out of your mouth.

These manifestations are designed to disable Christian effectiveness and/or hinder salvation.

The *familiar spirit* works in concert with the *lying spirit* to foist lies and half-truths resulting in deception in most things. It also combines with the influence of the *spirit of infirmity* to inflict and promote illnesses and diseases through inherited traits from your forefathers (*allergies, asthma, high blood pressure, obesity, optical problems, etc.*). This is a major spirit and is indeed one of the "root" spirits spoken of earlier.

LYING SPIRIT – vs. – SPIRIT of TRUTH

(1Kings 22:22-23; 2Kings 18:21-22).

When Jesus said in John 8:44 of the devil, *"He was a murderer from the beginning and does not stand in the truth, because there is no truth in him. When he speaks a falsehood, he speaks what is natural to him, for he is a liar [himself] and the father of lies and of all that is false."* He was addressing the assignment of the *lying spirit* decreed by Satan himself.

Because of this assignment, the *lying spirit* is prevalent in most demonization. Logic dictates that a *lying spirit* is involved with other evil spirits to deceive you, thereby preventing release and freedom from their intended bondage for you.

Manifestations of the *lying spirit* are manifold. It offers vigorous and continuous condemnation, strong delusions and exaggerations that embrace partial or half-truths. There will be much evidence of hypocrisy, e.g. pretending to be one thing while actually being another. Other manifestations in a person under the influence of a *lying spirit* include outright lies or lying, wicked fantasies, inordinate flattery and evil manipulation of others. A person can also be filled with false guilt and blame concerning past actions or thoughts.

A *religious spirit* is basically a *lying spirit* attempting to substitute meaningless ritual and tradition for a living relationship with Almighty God. Legalism is a fruit of the *lying spirit* as well. Its repertoire includes deception and seduction.

The *lying spirit* is another of the major root spirits involved in demonization. The *lying spirit* is the counterpart of the *Spirit of Truth* mentioned specifically in John 14:17. *"And I will ask the Father, and He will give you another Comforter (Counselor, Helper, Intercessor, Advocate, Strengthener, and Standby), that He may remain with you forever — The Spirit of Truth, Whom the world cannot receive (welcome, take to its heart), because it does not see Him or know and recognize Him, for He lives with you [constantly] and will be in you."*

The <u>*Spirit of Truth*</u> is resident with you who are believers. Therefore, it is important to understand that you have within you, the remedy to the *lying spirit,* that is the *Spirit of Truth.*

Recognize and apply the *Spirit of Truth* to any 'sin doors' you have opened, cast out *the lying spirit* in the Name of Jesus, and walk in truth.

ANTICHRIST SPIRIT – vs. – SPIRIT OF CHRIST

"And every spirit that does not acknowledge and confess that Jesus Christ has come in the flesh [but would annul, destroy, sever, disunite Him] is not of God [does not proceed from Him]. This [non-confession] is the [spirit] of the antichrist, [of] which you heard that it was coming, and now it is already in the world. Little children, you are of God [you belong to Him] and have [already] defeated and overcome them [the agents of the antichrist], because He Who lives in you is greater (mightier) than he who is in the world." (1John 4:3-4)

The above scripture describes the efforts of the *antichrist spirit:* to annul, destroy, sever, discredit and disunite the body of Christ. The prefix "anti" means counter to, opposite or against or instead of; therefore, antichrist is against or opposite to, or instead of, Christ.

Christ is the Greek word for The Anointed One ~ He Who was chosen by Yahweh to rule and reign in heaven and on earth for eternity. The Hebrew word for the same person is Messiah [The Anointed One].

The anointing of the Anointed One is resident upon and available *within* believers who ask and receive it. This anointing carries with it power to perform miraculous acts, discern good and evil spirits and further the work of Jesus the Christ on this earth.

It is no wonder that the enemy counterfeits and perpetuates the opposite spirit to the Christ in order to annul, sever, destroy and disunite His body. In essence, the *antichrist spirit* is against all things of Christ or His anointing.

Think of the things that destroy or dilute the anointing of God ~ anger, disunity, confusion, interruption, deception and compromise to name a few.

The manifestation of the *antichrist spirit* is to oppose holy doctrine, Deity in all its forms and promote victory for the spirit of the world. It attempts to replace or exchange the influence of the Living God in believers' lives with its own agenda. The *antichrist spirit* claims and attempts to use authority not granted. It evens suggests and substitutes other avenues for the atonement of the cross. Legalism and its bondage, in things both spiritual and natural, are constant manifestations of the *antichrist spirit*. This includes seduction of a person(s) into error, deception, unholiness and impurity. The *antichrist spirit* is a destroying spirit and drains away all efforts toward holiness, anointing and Christ-like qualities.

SPIRIT OF FEAR — vs. — FAITH

"The fear of man brings a snare, but whoever leans on, trusts in, and puts his confidence in the Lord is safe and set on high." (Proverbs 29:25) *"For God did not give us a spirit of fear (of cowardice, of craven and cringing and fawning fear), but [He has given us a spirit] of power*

Fear in all forms is the description of the *spirit of fear*. Fear of the unknown, fear of the known, fear of failure, fear of rejection, fear of trying, etc. The *spirit of fear* grips your soul like a vice, squeezing the life of freedom from you, rendering you helpless and impotent. These are not the normal cautionary pauses or the reluctance to act when facing something new. It is instead, a complete bondage to crippling fear resulting in metal "lock-down" when facing decisions and choices.

Manifestation of the *spirit of fear* includes hypercritical reactions and extremes in negative opinion. Judgementalism concerning someone's actions, words and appearance is yet another facet of this spirit's influence.

Selfishness, self-consciousness, low self-esteem and insecurity are also symptoms of the *spirit of fear*. Many phobias and neurosis find their origins in the *spirit of fear's* playground.

One of the end results of the *spirit of fear* is the manifestation of the *dumb and deaf spirit*. Fear is the enemy and destroyer of faith, making it an enemy of both God and man. Study and apply the principles of faith (*discussed at length in chapter 2*) in order to defeat the counterfeit, the *spirit of fear*.

The only appropriate fear is the wholesome fear mixed with love, respect and reverence of Almighty God.

DUMB AND DEAF SPIRIT
— vs. —
GODLY KNOWLEDGE AND REVELATION

This spirit is also described as the *dumb and blind spirit* in Matthew 12:22 and as the *spirit of stupor* in Romans 11:8. Mark 9:25 mentions this spirit as the *dumb and deaf spirit,* and gives Jesus' answer to the disciples' question, *"Why could not we drive it out?"* which was *"This kind cannot be driven out by anything but prayer and fasting."* This is the wording of the parallel passage in Matthew 17: 21. The spirit in verse 15 was referred to only as *epilepsy,* but in light of the parallel reference is identified as the same *dumb and deaf spirit.*

The *dumb and deaf spirit* has certain characteristics and traits. Among them are seizures and an inability to hear or see spiritual truths. Some forms of schizophrenia, insanity, lunacy and multiple personalities are other ways this spirit manifests itself. The *dumb and deaf spirit* also initiates even some stuttering, palsy and related speech or hearing problems. This spirit often resorts to "spiritual blackmail" and encourages believers under its attack to "Let's Make a Deal" bargains with God. It begins with "If you don't do this or follow what I say, I'll..." The *dumb and deaf spirit* works together with the *spirit of fear* and the *lying spirit* to conquer your free will and produce bondage.

This spirit is in opposition to God's knowledge and revelation, and will engage in all manners of devices to circumvent you from receiving such knowledge and revelation. It will appeal to your mind and logic, urging you to believe that the knowledge and revelation from God is nothing more than superstitious imagination containing simplistic explanations. This spirit presents Biblical truths as not being relevant for today's world, or it might suggest, "That dream (or vision) you thought was from God was nothing more than just too much pizza before going to bed."

Since the *dumb and deaf spirit's* main assignment is to obscure godly revelation and insight from you, there is difficulty in casting it out. Jesus said, this kind cannot be driven out except by prayer [by asking and receiving what God says concerning this spirit] and fasting [by denying the human impulses to conquer the *dumb and deaf spirit* through fleshly or natural resources].

SPIRIT OF BONDAGE
— vs. —
FREEDOM or THE SPIRIT OF ADOPTION

"For [the Spirit which] you have now received [is] not a spirit of slavery to put you once more in bondage to fear, but you have received the Spirit of adoption [the Spirit producing son-ship] in the [bliss of] which we cry, Abba (Father)! Father! The Spirit Himself [thus] testifies together with our own spirit, [assuring us] that we are children of God." (Romans 8:15-16) *"He must correct his opponents with courtesy and gentleness, in the hope that God may grant that they will repent and come to know the Truth [that they will perceive and recognize and become accurately acquainted with and acknowledge it]. And may they come to their senses [and] escape out of the snare of the devil, having been held captive by him, [henceforth] to do His [God's] will."* (2 Timothy 2:25-26)

The *spirit of bondage* is mostly self-explanatory because of its name: bondage in all forms. The *spirit of bondage* is Satan's counterfeit of several positive spirits created by God; among these is the *Spirit of adoption.*

Bondage can be either or both physical and soulish. Physical bondage can exist through addictions, unholy appetites and/or soulish bondage through mental, emotional and willful practices. Bondage of addiction and unholy appetites includes tobacco, opiates, alcohol, food and sexual or pornographic activity.

Mental and emotional bondage includes all ranges of problems of the psyche. Avarice, uninhibited ambition, and a driving, inordinate desire for gain or honor, position and recognition, power or money are other manifestations of the *spirit of bondage.* Any compulsive activity or mind-set that binds or limits your freedom is a function of this spirit.

The sense of being abandoned by God, family, friends, etc. is a key piece of evidence that the *spirit of bondage* is present.

The only effective remedy to this type of bondage is the *Spirit of adoption* provided by your relationship with the Lord Jesus Christ. By the *Spirit of adoption,* you are released from the bondage of seeking and depending on some other source to provide the feelings and facts of acceptance. You may choose instead, to depend on the truth of being chosen and accepted (adopted, if you will) by God through Christ Jesus.

You are then free to accept responsibility for your own actions and not place blame on someone or something else. There are no performance standards to achieve or need to otherwise "prove" yourself. This releases you into the true sense of freedom through repentance. So choose now to release control of your life to the One Who will rule with your best interests in mind.

PERVERSE SPIRIT — vs. — WORSHIP

"The Lord has mingled a spirit of perverseness, error, and confusion within her; [her leaders] have caused Egypt to stagger in all her doings, as a drunken man staggers in his vomit." (Isaiah 19:14)

"But Saul, who is also called Paul, filled with and controlled by the Holy Spirit, looked steadily at [Elymas] and said, You master in every form of deception and recklessness, unscrupulousness, and wickedness, you son of the devil, you enemy of everything that is upright and good, will you never stop perverting and making crooked the straight paths of the Lord and plotting against His saving purposes?" (Acts 13:9-10)

From the passage in Isaiah above, God names and gives a brief description of the *perverse spirit* regarding punishment upon Egypt in ancient days. A more complete description of the *perverse spirit* is given in Acts 13.

The incident occurs after a false prophet named Bar-Jesus [Elymas], a wizard, sorcerer and false prophet on the pretext of hearing the Gospel, tried to prevent the pro-consul of the island of Cyprus from accepting salvation. Paul spoke to the *perverse spirit* and struck the man blind by the power of God. After this the pro-consul became a believer.

The *perverse spirit* attempts to usurp authority by illegally seizing the right to all forms of purity, righteousness and divine worship. It twists purity, righteousness and divine worship into a caricature of their true forms and presents them (through man's rationalizations) as acceptable alternatives to God's intents and purposes.

Some of the manifestations of the *perverse spirit* are lust, sexual perversion, homosexuality, lesbianism, pornography, idolatry, witchcraft, occultism, stubbornness, rebellion and untrustworthiness.

These manifestations are to supplant divine worship. They are designed to become substitutes for the thrill of euphoric, happy and joyful manifestations of true worship of God, which is what we should 'fill the house' with after deliverance is achieved.

SPIRIT OF JEALOUSY [ENVY]
— vs. —
UNITY [LOVE, PEACE]

"And if the spirit of jealousy comes upon him and he is jealous and suspicious of his wife who has defiled herself — or if the spirit of jealousy comes upon him and he is jealous and suspicious of his wife though she has not defiled herself —." (Numbers 5:14)

"And so, since they did not see fit to acknowledge God or approve of Him or consider Him worth the knowing, God gave them over to a base and condemned mind to do things not proper or decent but loathsome, until they were filled (permeated and saturated) with every kind of unrighteousness, iniquity, grasping and covetous greed, and malice. [They were] full of envy and jealousy, murder, strife, deceit and treachery, ill will and cruel ways. [They

were] secret backbiters and gossipers, slanderers, hateful to and hating God, full of insolence, arrogance, [and] boasting; inventors of new forms of evil, disobedient and undutiful to parents. [They were] without understanding, conscienceless and faithless, heartless and loveless [and] merciless." (Romans 1:28-31)

The fruit of the *spirit of jealousy* are accurately listed in the above passage in Romans. These are counterfeit to the unity and love desired and offered by God to His children. Again the opposites of the listed items are the correct influences with which to 'fill the house' when exorcising this root with its fruit.

SPIRIT OF INFIRMITY
—vs. —
HEALTH OR WHOLENESS

"And there was a woman there who for eighteen years had an infirmity caused by a spirit (a demon of sickness). (Luke 13:11)

When facing sickness or illness (yours or another's) in any form, ask God if this is from the devil. If you do not receive an answer of 'yes,' proceed to use remedies through physicians and medicine. If you receive an answer of "Yes, it is from the enemy" then ask God "How do You want me to deal with it?" Many times God will direct you to engage in a spiritual battle with a certain spirit then stand in faith for the healing. At other times God will have you engage in spiritual warfare while seeking medical aid through doctors and medication. Using medical aid in no way indicates a lack of faith on your part. You are obeying what you hear God saying to you.

Immunity is the ability of living tissue to resist and overcome invading infections. Ask God for His immunity for your body from invading evil forces of infirmity in whichever form they appear, then obey His instructions.

Some of the manifestations of the *spirit of infirmity* are frailty and lingering, deep-seated health or mental disorders. Chronic respiratory infections, arthritis and allergies, fever and general feelings of ill health are other forms of this spirit's presence. This is not to say that these conditions must always be a result of this spirit.

Since Adam's fall, man has been sentenced to die physically. However, God said in Genesis 6:3, "...*But his days shall yet be 120 years.*" The life expectancy of man in the USA is somewhere between 76-80 years (nowhere near the 120). Many things done and not done in current lifestyles can contribute to the early demise of man. It is important for you to let God show you ways to prolong your life here on earth so you can share the gospel with those not yet 'born-again' and make disciples of believers after their conversion.

Satan has used the *spirit of infirmity* to increase the death rate among mankind. You need to ask and obey God's leading to a more healthy existence against the onslaught of the devil as seen in today's eating, drinking and pollution embracing trends.

SPIRIT OF HEAVINESS — vs. — PRAISE AND JOY

"To appoint unto them that mourn in Zion, to give them beauty for ashes, the oil of joy for mourning, the garment of praise for the spirit of heaviness; that they

might be called the trees of righteousness, the planting of the Lord, that He might be glorified." (Isaiah 61:3)

The mission of the *spirit of heaviness* is to prevent anything that glorifies God. Its manifestations are designed to rob your joy then produce its evil fruit within you. The *spirit of heaviness* works in conjunction with the *spirit of infirmity* to focus your attention on your circumstances rather than God and His provisions for you.

This spirit wants you to make a comparison with how happy or unhappy you are, always against an impossible standard of measure.

Remember that happiness has its seat in the soulish realm and depends on *outward* conditions and circumstances for its fulfillment. However, outward conditions and circumstances are always temporary and changing, continually subjecting you to cyclic bouts of 'highs" and "lows."

The only true remedy is to substitute joy whose seat is in the spiritual realm where there is no dependence on outward situations for its fulfillment. God can make your joy permanent and eliminate the roller-coaster ride of emotion and logic.

Psalm 100:4 states *"Enter into His gates with thanksgiving and into His courts with praise!"*

The progression is first, thanksgiving then praise. Worship will follow and joy will be the result. This will defeat the *spirit of heaviness.*

JEZEBEL and AHAB SPIRIT

The combination of the *Jezebel spirit* and the *Ahab spirit* are opposite sides of the same coin. Where one is present, there is a great probability the other exists as well. These are strong, mighty spirits and often hide in the shadows of other lesser spirits present in the demonization of individuals. Jezebel is usually relegated to females and Ahab to males, but due to the 'role reversing' influences present in these spirits, either gender can be affected.

The story of King Ahab and his wife Jezebel is told in 1 Kings, chapters 17,18, 19, 21 & 22. The demise of Jezebel is detailed in 2Kings 9: 30-37.

Perhaps the best summary of the *Jezebel and Ahab spirits* is contained in this scripture: *"For there was no one who sold himself to do evil in the sight of the Lord as did Ahab, incited by his wife Jezebel."* (1Kings 21:25)

This is a spirit of usurpation (*to seize another's power, rights or possessions illegally*). Its single objective is to grasp the power, rights and possessions that are rightfully yours by illegal and deceptive means. This is usually accomplished in harmony with the *spirit of fear* and the *familiar spirit* to intimidate and/or seduce you into surrendering your legal authority to its control.

Manifestations of the *Jezebel spirit* include seizing and holding the rights and power of another by illegal forces of intimidation, deception and control.

Domination by innuendo, manipulation and intimidation; destruction of self-confidence and self-acceptance by lying and deceitfulness are other manifestations of this spirit. The absence of submission to authority plus gender role reversal are other attributes of this evil spirit. The rise in radical feminism, lesbianism and homosexuality are also its products. The verbal and visual diminishing of traditional male and female functions and appearance, by substituting unisex and 'role reversing' trends, are also goals of the *spirit of Jezebel*.

The *Ahab spirit* has as its manifestation the abdication of rightful authority, responsibility and gender role. It promotes a weak-willed and easily intimidated attitude filled with selfishness, laziness and fear of responsibility. This type personality is often called 'hen-pecked,' 'weak-willed,' 'effeminate.' Men suffering from this influence often rise to positions of prominence only to be controlled and intimidated by a female (usually wife, mother, sister, etc.).

As with all demonization, the remedy of submitting to God with the whole heart, discerning of spirits as necessary, then resisting the exposed devil (casting out) resulting in his fleeing from us.

As stated in the beginning of this chapter demonization is a serious and crippling soul storm to be faced by believers. If the understanding presented is grasped and applied, a believer in Jesus the Christ can successfully conquer such 'blue northers' and truly be known as a "storm-proof" child of the King.

CHAPTER TWELVE

THE NECCESSITY OF CHANGE

Why is change necessary?

Solutions to the 'blue northers' of soul storms cannot be achieved without *change* in some form. This change may be as simple as a change of perspective or as disrupting as changing geographic location. Change in any form is *always* difficult. There are no exceptions. This is one of the reasons *you* resist change so much. Change can be from *within* or *without,* but will always include the exercise of *choice* and the endurance of some *pain.*

These choices may be voluntary on your part or sometimes forced through situations and circumstances. This pain of change may be merely the sting of nostalgia associated with the exchange of environment as a new growth pattern emerges.

For example, the emotional effect (or pain) results from the change involving a physical move to a new locality. There is distress experienced in giving up old friends and acquaintances for new ones and/or moving away from an old familiar place into a new, unfamiliar one.

The pain of change may also be an emotional upheaval of knowing something (a relationship or situation) is now over or completed. Such an example as leaving home to go away to college, graduation from college, leaving old familiar friends, changing employment, divorce, the breakup with a sweetheart, the death of a loved one, etc.

During my years of employment I had very few jobs. Consequently, I did not face the chaos of moving very often. However, when I did change cities for a new job, it was fraught with the adjustments and pain of change both for my family and myself. The good-byes to familiar friends and familiar surroundings were replaced with hellos and adjustment to unfamiliar ones.

I can say with assurance that every move made was one with positive results due to the growth and changes in my life. Not all the moves were comfortable. In fact I don't believe *any* were comfortable. Sometimes the salary I needed was available only if I moved. Sometimes circumstances dictated that I move for the emotional and spiritual well being of my family.

However, the discipline I learned as a result of each new position promoted a maturing of my whole being. I could then become more assured of who I was while the skill and ability with which to perform my assignment increased proportionally.

It was through one of these moves that I finally became a believer in the Lord Jesus Christ. Think of the eternal benefit of this change with its pain in my life. As I think back on it, there was nothing comfortable or pleasant in the circumstances leading up to my decision. In fact, quite the opposite was true.

This change occurred during a time in which I found myself unable to look anywhere else and unable to depend on anyone else except the Living God. All the while God Himself was orchestrating the events and circumstances necessary for drawing my spirit to Him. What a marvelous Savior!

This would be an example from my own life of how Roman 8:28 really works. *"We are assured and know that [God being a partner in their labor] all things work together and are [fitting into a plan] for good to and for those who love God and are called according to [His] design and purpose."*

God brought and allowed the exact mixture of pressure and chaos necessary for both my wife and I to turn our lives over to the loving hands of our Lord Jesus. He took all the negatives occurring in our lives during that time and worked them together for good as He called us into His purposes and plans.

Since change also means leaving something familiar and embracing something new or foreign, it is met with a combination of fear, dread and apprehension. There is always fear of the unknown and unfamiliar. Without a basic foundation of faith in Christ Jesus, these unknowns and unfamiliars can become quite devastating.

On the contrary, if you know Him Who holds tomorrow and all that is not known or familiar to you, you can face change with trust. God will not lead you anywhere He will not provide and prosper you and will accompany you with His Presence.

Changes within and without

Change *within* a person is usually one of an attitude or a perspective that affects one's choices. Change occurring *outside* a person can often mean the evolution of circumstances and situations creating a different set of stimuli, which *affect* our choices and responsibilities. Pressures build up within and without causing one to *choose* to change.

One of the changes *within* a person must be the change of the *mindset* or *habits of thought*. A mindset means that when confronted with a particular problem, you routinely deduct or arrive at a solution with a decision based on prior habits of reason or deduction you have developed.

When a permanent change occurs in your life (*whether that permanent change is a result of your own choices or those created by environment or circumstances*) it is important that you choose a change in your thinking as you approach each new situation.

The old way doesn't work in the new environment or at least doesn't apply anymore. This is a change from *within*.

You must stop and change the 'stinking thinking' (*that is the way the world thinks or the way the devil wants you to think*) and become a 'light thinker.' Many times when the Bible speaks of light it is referring to revelation (light) from God.

What I mean by 'light thinking' is that the thoughts you choose to entertain must be thoughts based on the light (revelation) of God or what the Word of God reveals concerning this subject. This is so simple, but is missed by most believers. It is necessary for you to change your old habits or old methods of thinking.

From another viewpoint, this 'stinking thinking' is having *your* thinking and deductions grounded on *your* senses or feelings. As long as decisions are based on your feelings, you will be deluded at worst; while at best, you will be at the mercy of your senses. Decisions must be based on what God's Word says concerning situations and circumstances.

To base the solutions to soul storms on anything other than what is said in God's Word is to yield to the *captivity of circumstance*. During these times, the maturity level of your walk as a believer is undergoing the refinement of change.

What do you mean by the captivity of circumstance?

Often the circumstances you find yourself in dictate a very different action from what you would have originally planned *before* those circumstances occurred. The boundaries and consequent limits imposed by circumstances are what I refer to as the *'captivity of circumstance.'* These boundaries are the *limits* to what you can and cannot do. Just like walls of a jail cell these circumstances hold us in captivity to certain limits.

Many centuries ago when the people of Israel had been transported to Babylon after the successful conquest and fall of Jerusalem (*which God had orchestrated*), they found themselves mired in the *'captivity of circumstances'* contained in the Babylonian captivity. God chose to speak to His people through the prophet Jeremiah concerning this captivity.

"Thus says the Lord of hosts, the God of Israel, to all the captives whom I have caused to be carried into exile from Jerusalem to Babylon: Build yourselves houses and dwell in them; plant gardens and eat the fruit of them. Take wives and have sons and daughters; take wives for your sons and give your daughters in marriage, that they may bear sons and daughters; multiply there, and do not be diminished. And seek (inquire for, require, and request) the peace and welfare of the city to which I have caused you to be carried away captive; and pray to the Lord for it, for in the welfare of [the city in which you live] you will have welfare." (Jeremiah 29:4-7)

A paraphrase of this is almost the same as "Bloom where I have planted you." This is a case where the circumstances cause us to affect a change in our approach to *where* we live as well as the *way* we live there.

In the midst of every circumstance, God speaks of continuing to serve Him and giving ourselves to the normal assignments in fruitful living, especially praying for the welfare of the place in which we find ourselves. This type of change requires an adjustment in our thinking based on location and authority. It also allows us to overcome many limitations in the captivity of circumstance.

The change of salvation

The greatest change desired in you is that being wrought by the Holy Spirit to conform you into the image of the Lord Jesus Christ (see Romans 8:29). Though each person is indeed uniquely individual, there is only one assignment commanded for us all ~ *become transformed into the image of the Christ.* The degree of change necessary is dictated by how *unlike* Jesus we find ourselves.

This change will in no way diminish your singular individual personality, but will instead allow God to develop you into a unique replica of Christ that exactly fits your profile. Isn't that amazing, a change that allows you to become your true self and still look, act and decide as Jesus!

Let's explore several ways change is available and suitable for you in this process of conformity to the image of Jesus.

As stated earlier in Chapter 1, when salvation occurs, you become a new creature (*species*) in the spiritual realm or spiritual dimension of your life. However, your soul (*mind, will and emotions*) and your container (*body*) remain basically in the same state as they were before you accepted Christ as your Savior and Lord.

The nuclear part of you (*your spirit*) has been totally, completely and permanently changed. This has set in motion the equation for your whole being (spirit, soul and body) finally becoming permanently changed as well. The major difference in the two types of change (*spirit change and soul change*) is that the process of changing the soul is more tedious, toilsome and time-consuming than the changing of the spirit. However, the price paid by Jesus was the same for both cases (*man's spirit change and man's soulish change*).

The reason I have omitted referring to changing the body is that the body follows the dictates of the soul. Whatever the soul wants ~ physically, mentally or emotionally ~ will affect the body as well. When the choices of the soul chose or accept the ingredients of addiction (alcohol, drugs, perversion, etc.) the body follows the dictates of the soul that result in its addictive state.

This in no way overlooks the necessity of affecting the healing of the body. Jesus healed the sick, maimed, blind, deaf and leprous. When the body is suffering under the influence of illnesses, you are to pray for and expect, through faith, God's healing virtue to manifest the change of healing. It is important to remember that *"without faith it is impossible to please God."* This is why it is important that you keep seeking and obtaining God's will before you make your decisions. You can then have faith (the ingredient that pleases God) applied and operating in all your decisions and choices.

It is also a fact that the body of man is dying, and will only be completely renewed when you go to heaven or receive your glorified body after the return of the Lord Jesus Christ to the earth. However, it is not necessary for you to be sick or ill in order to die.

In summary, the change of salvation is designed to bring total conformity to the image of our Lord Jesus the Christ.

James Ryle, a pastor in Colorado, preached a sermon I heard that expressed the following. Its message has been most beneficial to me in my walk with the Lord.

Healthy things grow!
Growing things change!
and
Changing things challenge!

The tremendous truth contained in the three lines above will aid you in the conquering of the soul storms blowing into your life in the guise of changes.

Whether you are talking about plants, animals or human beings, the first statement, *Healthy things grow,* is true and applicable. If you are healthy, you grow. When you cease or fail to grow, you die or begin to die.

The truth of the first statement leads to the logic of the second, *Growing things change!* The very word 'growth' means change. You change in size, shape, age and purpose. You change in order to grow and bear fruit. Some changes are attractive while some are down right ugly! But pretty or ugly, things (and people) change.

The last statement is very profound, *changing things challenge!* Humans are mostly resistant to change. We like the familiar and the routine. Change is unknown, and humans fear and resist the unknown. Surprises are not always pleasant or welcome. Change usually means discomfort in some form, and we don't like to be uncomfortable (do we?).

The biggest reason for resisting change is that we are unable to *control* it. We humans like to be *in charge*! If this principle is not understood it can cause a great deal of anguish in your life. When you are healthy, you grow;

when you grow, you change and when you change, you challenge. This applies to *all human relationships* ~ friendships, romances, marriages, parenting, employment, church life, politics, etc.

God's grace causes change!

One other thought concerning the matter of God's grace. Grace has been defined in various ways; *"undeserved favor of God"* is perhaps the most prevalent. There is a much deeper application than just *favor*, which has limited meaning in English use.

The Greek word used for grace is *charis*, which has various uses. Gifting and power to live God's way are close to the Greek meaning in English. This will give you power to face and adapt to change. It sometimes means only God's grace can help you endure this that you are going through.

God's grace is for free and for all. It cannot be earned or deserved. Grace is the foundation of faith and the power to complete faith (there is also the power to live God's way). You must realize and accept this fact on a personal, intimate basis. His grace is the foundation of *your* faith and contains the power to complete *your* faith.

God's grace can be compared to the ocean and your faith to a bucket. Since the bucket leaks (*doesn't it?*) and is in constant need of refilling, it is important for you to continue your journey to the source (God's grace) for replenishment. There is much more grace than you can carry or exhaust by use. You can however, increase the size of your bucket (your capacity to contain faith) by continuous exercise. But there will always be much more than you need for all your insufficiency.

You and I as recipients can have *but one response to God's grace.* That is the response of *thankfulness.* This also illustrates the accuracy of the Psalms, which declares we are to approach God with thankfulness that evolves into praise. *"Enter into His gates with thanksgiving and a thank offering and into His courts with praise! Be thankful and say so to Him, bless and affectionately praise His name! For the Lord is good; His mercy and loving-kindness are everlasting, His faithfulness and truth endure to all generations."* (Psalm 100:4-5)

Charis is also used in the familiar word *Charisma,* which is translated from Greek into English as the word, *gift.* It is fascinating to me that the very word for grace is also related to the word translated as gift. This would mean that the *gifts* I receive from God are those that are also filled with His *grace.*

Instead of resisting change, you must learn that to healthy things, change is necessary. As changes occur, accept their challenges by receiving God's grace in adapting and adjusting to those changes. The reward is to receive more changes and the cycle repeats.

If you will learn this simple lesson, God can make the soul storms of 'change' in your life, opportunities for growth, perseverance and maturity.

CHAPTER THIRTEEN

RELATIONSHIPS

Another painful storm of the soul is found in relationships. Some of the most crippled persons on earth are so maimed because of relationships gone sour. Unless answers are found to alleviate the problems in relationships, the believer is unable to fully enjoy the abundant life of which Jesus spoke.

The root word from which relationship is taken is the word, **relate**.

Relate by definition means: to bring into logical or natural association; to have connection, relation or reference; to interact with others in a significant or coherent way.

Although I feel most of the readers have a general concept of what relationships consist, I need to be a bit more specific to explain my approach to them. A relationship is a connection between two or more persons by blood, marriage, associations and dealings for personal, business or diplomatic interchange. Let's identify and list some of the relationships that affect us.

- Relationship of parent, child and family — blood or adoption related.
- Marriage — legal or common law.
- Body of Christ — related through regeneration and 'new birth' in Jesus.
- Acquaintance or friend.

- Employer/employee.

Now to take some time and explore the Seventh Commandment and its correlation to relationships. *"Thou shall not commit adultery."* (Exodus 20:14)

Many are not aware of how serious adultery is or of how frequently it occurs. I will go so far as to say adultery is the basis of a breakdown in all relationships.

Why is adultery so devastating?

Examine the origin of the word adultery and its meaning. Then observe how your selfish thoughts, actions and behavior manifest that meaning in your life. You can begin to see why it is so important to guard yourself from all forms of adultery.

The root word to adultery is **adulterate,** and adulterate means to make impure, spurious or inferior by adding extraneous or improper ingredients. (*Spurious means false, illegitimate, lacking validity or authenticity.*) Adulterate also means to make similar in appearance but unlike in function or structure.

Therefore, to adulterate a relationship is to make it impure, false or illegitimate. A counterfeit, if you will. This coincides with what Jesus called the Scribes and Pharisees: pretenders, hypocrites, and play-actors (Luke 6,13, Matthew 23). Jesus described them in that fashion because the Scribes and Pharisees were making a big pretense for appearance sake, but functioned quite differently from that appearance. In other words, adulterating their positions and relationships.

Allow me to connect this concept with Scripture before proceeding further.

In Paul's letter to the Ephesians, he outlines the role of wives, husbands, children, fathers, servants and masters. In the center of his discussion, after the admonition to husbands and wives, he refers to Genesis 2:24, *"Therefore a man shall leave his father and his mother and shall be joined to his wife, and the two shall become one flesh."* Paul used a different introduction to this verse by stating *"For this reason a man shall leave his father and his mother etc...."*

The phrase *'this reason'* refers to the mystery of how the 'one flesh' of marriage parallels our relationship as the Christ's body (church) relates with Christ and also is 'one flesh' with Him. *"For this reason a man shall leave his father and his mother and shall be joined to his wife, and the two shall become one flesh. This mystery is very great, but I speak concerning [the relation of] Christ and the church."* (Ephesians 5:31-32)

Since sexual intimacy is to be conducted only within the bounds of marriage, sexual intimacy under any other circumstance is either fornication or adultery.

In the passages above, God explains why there is such gravity to sexual activity outside marriage. When your body is united to anyone sexually, you become one flesh with them. This means you take upon and within yourself all the characteristics, weaknesses and propensity toward sin that is resident in the person to whom you joined yourself. This will also include those with whom he/she has been joined in sexual union before you. Marriage is the only safe place for intimacy to occur.

The church is described as the body of Christ (1Corinthians 12:27; Colossians 1:18). If you are one flesh with the one you marry in the natural setting, then being married to Christ will make you one flesh with Him. You are *everything He is* and are *becoming conformed* to everything He is. As a believer who has been adopted into the family of God and a member of the body of Christ, you are in fact engaged to Christ. Therefore, a comparison of marriage and the church's relationship with Jesus is more easily understood.

In Jewish custom and tradition, when a man and woman are engaged or betrothed, they are, in the eyes of Jewish law, married even though the physical union has not been consummated. The physical union of the Bride of Christ will not occur until His final return, but until that time you are His betrothed and are married to your Lord.

Because of your relationship with Christ, anytime you adulterate an earthly relationship in which you are currently engaged you commit adultery against the Person and principles of Christ.

For example, If you break your word to another person concerning an obligation you have made with them, you are misrepresenting Christ. Why? Since you are a believer engaged to be married to Jesus and one flesh with Him, you represent and reflect Jesus and all that He is to others. The popular phrase *"What Would Jesus Do?"* is very appropriate.

To the world that knows you are a believer, what you *do* is what *they* think Jesus would do also. Jesus does not break His word and when you break yours, you adulterate your word by failing to abide by it.

This explains why I said the breaking of the Seventh Commandment applies to all relationships.

What are the stages in a relationship?

There are several progressive steps in the evolution of relationships. Some of these steps are applicable in all relationships while other steps are 'stand alone' ones for only certain kinds of relations. The best example is that of marriage and reproduction. Let's list the steps then discuss each briefly.

- Introduction or first time meeting
- Orientation and familiarization
- Compatibility, affinity, and attractiveness
- Commitment, promise, or contract
- Covenant or vows (can also include contract)

(the following apply to marriages)

- Intimacy
- Conception
- Gestation
- Travail
- Birth

Introduction or first time meeting.

Every human relationship must have this step. We are introduced and /or meet for the first time. Sometimes, as in the case of employment the meeting involves answering an advertisement for employment, being recommended by someone else, etc.

In the case of marriage, there is also a first time meeting ~ sometime by introduction ~ sometime a chance meeting. There is usually a long distance between a first time meeting and a marriage, but it always begins first with a meeting.

Even in a family situation, a child will be seen or introduced for the first time and thus begins the relationship. This can happen even before birth while the child is observed to move within the womb.

As this applies to the church (the body of Christ), you must individually meet Jesus for the first time in order to begin a relationship with Him. Upon your acceptance of His invitation to relate with Him, you are inducted into the family of God (Body of Christ).

Contrary to all efforts on our behalf, unless God draws one to Himself, there will be no introduction. God will use human effort, but it is His grace that accomplishes our introduction to Jesus. *"For it is by grace that you are saved through faith."* (Ephesians 2:8)

Orientation and familiarization

Sometimes the relationship begins first, then the orientation and familiarization occurs. Other times the reverse is true.

This is also the stage where you determine if you can be friends or not.

The danger of entering into a relationship without the orientation and familiarization is that you oftentimes get into something you didn't count on or would not have entered into had you known certain things were involved.

This is especially important in a marriage setting. Since you are to be married for life, you and your future spouse need to know as much as possible about each other. Many marriages fail for this very reason; you don't know each other and the details of each other's personalities. This step is initiated here and continues throughout the length of the relationship.

Compatibility, Affinity and Attractiveness

In this step you discover if the original attractiveness or lack thereof remains. Occasionally, you find the original attraction has faded or waned, and no longer draws you toward that other person. It is important for you to find out the areas where you are compatible, as well as areas where you don't see eye-to-eye. You can discover if you have a natural, mutual, personal attraction or an inherent similarity as to outlooks on issues of life.

This period in a relationship must be long enough to see if your differences are too much for you to continue or not. This might be called the dating part of a relationship.

Commitment, Promise, or Contract

This step might be called the engagement phase. This is where you make commitment or promise to continue the relationship. (In the business world this is sometimes known as the end of the probationary period).

By this time, the two persons contemplating marriage are pretty sure they want to enter into this lifetime relationship with each other. They probably have given or received an engagement ring, even set a target date for the marriage. This is also a time in which to determine if there are any reasons to wait longer or continue in this endeavor.

Covenant, Vows and Oath

The decision is now made to enter into covenant with each party through vows and/or an oath. In marriage this is for life, in other relationships there are time limits that are mostly less than a lifetime in duration.

I have waited until this point to draw a comparison in our relationship with Jesus. From the preceding steps of orientation & familiarization through compatibility, affinity and attractiveness into commitment and covenant, the relationship with Jesus is applicable. He makes Himself known to us through familiar examples (familiarization). Jesus helps us realize that we are certainly compatible with Him because we cannot be all that we are designed to become without His Presence in our lives (compatibility). The Lord requires from us a covenant and promise to Him, but also allows us to see the covenant He makes with us which far exceeds anything else in this world.

A covenant and/or contract with vows is known as the marriage ceremony. All of us know that a ceremony is the first step, and necessary, but does not make a marriage successful. This is where God's Presence in us aids us to endure the adjustments and compromise necessary to make and prepare a successful marriage.

Intimacy, Conception, Gestation, Travail and Birth

God plants within each of us the capacity to reproduce after our kind. This applies not only to the physical but the spiritual aspect of our life as well. In order to reproduce by birth that which is within us, there must first be intimacy.

Sexual expression within the confines of marriage is the deepest and most physical act of love in a human being. In the same manner worship allows the deepest spiritual expression of intimacy between a believer and his God. Psalms 115:8 declares, *"They who make idols are like them; so are all who trust in and lean on them."* This means you become like the idol(s) you worship. For this reason God has expressed He is a jealous God. He only wants you to have intimacy (worship) with Him.

I used to think that God was so insecure that He became jealous if I were to worship something or someone else instead of Him. The reason God is jealous is not for an emotional reason of His, but because of what adulterated worship does to man. Mankind becomes like what he worships. If man worships anything or anyone else but God, he becomes like them instead of Him. It would be a terrible thing to have the potential to become like God and toss it away to become something less.

In a spiritual sense, you commit adultery when you *substitute* some materialistic item, human relationship, worldly position of power, wealth or anything else *in place* of your worship of the Living God.

174

The passage below is a great truth concerning free will, slavery to sin and sinning with the body, as well as the seriousness of it.

"Everything is permissible (allowable and lawful) for me; but not all things are helpful (good for me to do, expedient and profitable when considered with other things). Everything is lawful for me, but I will not become the slave of anything or be brought under its power. Food [is intended] for the stomach and the stomach for food, but God will finally end [the functions of] both and bring them to nothing. The body is not intended for sexual immorality, but [is intended] for the Lord, and the Lord [is intended] for the body [to save, sanctify, and raise it again]. And God both raised the Lord to life and will also raise us up by His power. Do you not see and know that your bodies are members (bodily parts) of Christ (the Messiah)? Am I therefore to take the parts of Christ and make [them] parts of a prostitute? Never! Never! Or do you know and realize that when a man joins himself to a prostitute, he becomes one body with her? The two, it is written, shall become one flesh. But the person who is united with the Lord becomes one spirit with Him. Shun immorality and all sexual looseness [flee from impurity in thought, word, or deed]. Any other sin which man commits is one outside the body, but he who commits sexual immorality sins against his own body. Do you not know that your body is the temple (the very sanctuary) of the Holy Spirit Who lives within you, Whom you have received [as a gift] from God? You are not your own. You were bought with a price [purchased with preciousness and paid for, made His own]. So then, honor God and bring glory to Him in your body." (1Corinthinans 6:12-20)

To repeat, sexual intimacy is to be confined to marriage. To do otherwise is to commit fornication or adultery. Remember 'one flesh' occurs with any person to whom you join yourself in sexual activity. You become *all* that is present in each other's life. Within marriage this is desired and safe. Outside marriage it is devastating and deadly. God paid a great price for us all and you belong to him, not to your own free will.

Man's greatest power is the power to choose!
But you do not have the power to choose
the consequences of your choices.

The second step in the birth process is <u>conception</u>. We are commanded to be fruitful and multiply. Therefore, conception is the beginning of the fruit bearing and the multiplying process. The fruit you bear will be like that with which you join yourself. If you are united to anyone or anything other than God, your fruit will be ungodly. Your fruit contains the essence of the seed and the sperm (life). If the seed is anything other than that of God it will be adulterated from its potential.

The fruit you bear will be like
that with which you (worship or) join yourself.

Consider the passage from Proverbs. *"Drink waters out of your own cistern [of pure marriage relationship], and fresh running waters out of your own well. Should your offspring be dispersed abroad as water brooks in the streets? [Confine yourself to your own wife] let your children be for you alone, and not the children of strangers with you. Let your fountain [of human life] be blessed [with the rewards of fidelity], and rejoice in the wife of your youth. Let her be as the loving hind and pleasant doe [tender, gentle, attractive] — let her bosom satisfy you at all times, and always be transported with delight in her love. Why should you, my son, be infatuated with a loose woman, embrace the bosom of an outsider, and go astray? For the ways of man are directly before the eyes of the Lord, and He [Who would have us live soberly, chastely, and godly] carefully weighs all man's goings. His own iniquities shall ensnare the wicked man, and he shall be held with the cords of his sin. He will die for lack of discipline and instruction, and in the greatness of his folly he will go astray and be lost.* " (Proverbs 5:15-23)

The major emphasis in this passage is that of making the right choices (confine your desire to your mate), regardless of circumstances and receiving the rewards of fidelity. Realize that everything you do is before the eyes of the Lord. This will allow conceptions in your life that contains the sperm of God in them.

Gestation is the subsequent phase after conception. This is the period of carrying the developing offspring in the uterus after conception (pregnancy).

During this period of time the development of the unborn child is in progress. It is part of the child's growth, but it is protected growth until adequate maturity is achieved to the extent that physical birth takes place.

This can apply to mental conception and development of an idea as well. Children or ideas birthed before their due time can lead to limited success and danger. It is a time of change and discomfort, but is necessary in the growth process for optimum health of the child (or idea).

At the end of gestation there arrives a still more unpleasant phase known as travail. This is strenuous physical or mental exertion, also known as the labor of childbirth. With the advent of a child, idea or concept there must also be the travail of birthing. The good thing about travail is that when it is over and the child or idea is birthed, there is a great sense of satisfaction which occurs evaporating the memory of travail's strength and length.

Of course the last step in this process is the one of birth. At birth, the infant (or idea) is now breathing and functioning on its own. It is independent from its host, ready for growth into its potential. If the fruit is of God it will benefit those around it; if not there is rottenness and missed potential.

What is the difference between temptation and sin?

It is no sin to be tempted or have seductive and suggestive thoughts! It becomes a sin only when you entertain those thoughts. This gives way to fantasy and vain imaginings, which are sins of the mind. They can later evolve into actions of flirting, seduction and adultery.

To entertain a thought (or stimuli) of temptation is to allow the thought or other stimuli to hold the attention of the mind. It also means to extend hospitality toward, to harbor or maintain the temptation.

For example, when a tempting thought or scene occurs, you begin to consider through curiosity, jealousy, envy, and/or lust fulfilling and playing out the seductive conclusion of the thought or scene. This can occur in the workplace, at home, at school, at church or anywhere. The temptation can be toward anything by which you can be tempted: perversion, lust, greed, jealousy, envy, pride, etc. (you fill in any subject not mentioned).

As you entertain, harbor and maintain the temptation you give way to thought patterns of sin. Left unchecked and unconfessed, these thoughts give place to sinful behavior patterns that then become sin-filled addictions. Remember, to be tempted is not a sin.

Thought patterns can be broken easier than behavior habits. Habits of *behavior* are broken easier than *addictions*. Therefore, the earlier sin can be addressed the easier it is to overcome.

Listen to what Scripture teaches us about Jesus and His understanding of temptation. *"For we do not have a High Priest Who is unable to understand and sympathize and have a shared feeling with our weakness and infirmities and liability to the assaults of temptation, but One Who has been tempted in every respect as we are, yet without sinning. Let us then fearlessly and confidently and boldly draw near to the throne of grace (the throne of God's unmerited favor to us sinners), that we may receive mercy [for our failures] and find grace to help in good time for every need [appropriate help and well-timed help, coming just when we need it]."* (Hebrews 4:15-16)

A reminder:

> Healthy things grow!
> Growing things change!
> Changing things challenge!

A "blue norther" of soul storms is one of destroyed relationships with others. One of the reasons for the demise of relationships lies in not understanding and applying the truth of these three statements above. Let's continue to focus on the one relationship that is familiar, the relationship of marriage.

What is a healthy marriage?

If a marriage is healthy, it will *grow*. What is meant by a healthy marriage? Several things come to mind. One is the choice of having God in the center of each partner's life. To be **God-Centered** then becomes the common denominator for marriage health. It also helps explain the admonition of not becoming unequally yoked with unbelievers. *"Do not be unequally yoked with unbelievers [do not make mismated alliances with them or come under a different yoke with them, inconsistent with your faith]. For what partnership have right living and right standing with God with iniquity and lawlessness? Or how can light have fellowship with darkness?"* (2 Corinthians 6:14)

An illustration is made about how a healthy marriage resembles an equilateral triangle. The husband is represented by the lower left-hand angle, the wife by the lower right-hand angle while God resides at the upper angle of the triangle. As each spouse draws nearer to God (up their corresponding leg of the triangle), they also grow closer to each other (across the legs of the triangle). This becomes the secret of growing closer together to each other: draw near to God.

Another ingredient in a healthy marriage is <u>effective communication</u>. Notice I said *effective* communication. This means communicating so that each spouse *understands* the true meaning contained in the actions, words, body language, etc. of the other. Too many times marriage partners play psychological, emotional and verbal games with each other and fail miserably to effectively communicate.

Such things as inaccurate or misleading replies to questions like, "What's wrong, honey?" "What did I do to upset you?" "Why won't you speak to me or tell me what's wrong?"

Both men and women play the games of pouting, sulking, withdrawal, unforgiveness and revenge with each other. These result in responses of anger, rejection, retaliation, etc. that are all negatives to effective communication.

This raises the necessity of getting to know each other as well as possible *before* getting married and letting the effective process continue afterwards as well.

We must communicate in both honesty and love while using tact to approach the truth. Someone said, *"The truth told with ill intent is more deadly than all the lies you can invent."* Changes are occurring constantly, get to know the new (or changed) person constantly, too.

For example, a wife grows up in a family who showed much affection for each other through touching, hugging and kissing before leaving for work or school, etc. Her family also verbally said, *"I love you"* often. This is her example and model of knowing, feeling and proving that her family loved her.

On the other hand her husband grew up in a family who showed very little emotion. This lack of emotional expression was especially expected in its male members. Handshakes (with a few bear hugs) were the most demonstrative actions of love that were expressed. Words were very rare when expressing tender emotions for members of the family. His father did not talk much of his workplace and its accompanying problems. His mother and father did not physically or verbally demonstrate their love in front of the children. This was his model of marriage.

Think what terrible misunderstandings can occur if these two don't learn to communicate their true feelings and intentions toward each other. Again, get to know each other as well as possible *before* marriage and let this process continue every day afterwards.

Needless to say, if this couple does not get to know each other well before entering into the marriage, they will need major adjustments in each set of behaviors because of their diverse backgrounds. They are in for a rocky journey in their marriage until they can both adapt and change behavior so that effective communication can be established with each other. He must learn to express his emotions more openly, and she must not depend on behavior and words for the only confirmation of her husband's love for her.

This emphasizes the need for a couple to become *friends* before they become *lovers*. Physical involvement exhibits only one dimension of a person's personality and is not enough on which to base a good marriage. Many marriages have failed for just his reason. Friendship on the other hand, exhibits most all the personality sides of a person allowing each to observe and adjust to the dissimilar facets of one another.

Still another ingredient in a healthy marriage is that of trust. *Trust* must be practiced and displayed faithfully and consistently. *Trust* can be a great by-product of a relationship between friends and can grow into *trust* for a marriage as well. Jealousy has little chance to reign when *trust* is present. *Trust* is also necessary for addressing and resolving the rejections experienced between marriage partners. For a marriage to become healthy and grow there must be change and these changes will certainly challenge.

Growing closer to God on an individual basis
is the beginning of successful health
in all human relationships!

A marriage (or any human relationship, for that matter) is either growing closer to each other or growing farther apart. Remember the equilateral triangle referred to earlier.

Growing closer to God on an individual basis is the beginning of successful health in all human relationships.

Interests and ambitions, goals and objectives are not static but changing. As children arrive in marriage, a new set of adjustments must be made and changes will enter the picture.

Another ingredient to a healthy relationship and its changes is that of <u>commitment</u>. God demonstrated *commitment* by His covenant with mankind. Jesus, the Christ, became the bridge over which mankind can truly enter into a proper relationship with Abba, our Father. Jesus' death on the cross is the *commitment* God made with us to make our fellowship with Him possible.

This is our example; therefore, we must enter into relationships with *commitment*, both to each other and to the marriage relationship itself. The marriage vows taken are promises of our *commitment* before God to each other and to embrace changes that might occur (*in sickness and health, for richer or poorer, etc.*).

Many marriages are dissolved today because of a lack of *commitment*. Many other relationships are also lacking in the necessary *commitment* to the success of their continuing existence. This means the challenge of change was cause enough for the dissolution of a relationship.

A good relationship doesn't 'just happen.' It must be consistently reviewed and adjustments made to keep a relationship 'fine-tuned' and running smoothly. Challenges due to changes are to be expected, accepted and overcome in order for us to successfully become 'storm-proof' rather than just 'storm-free.' This too, is another solution to soul storms.

CHAPTER FOURTEEN

REACTION OR RESPONSE

Which Should I do, React or Respond?

Standing up in a soul storm you are facing may be as simple as learning to *respond* rather than to *react*.

I remember learning the difference between *reacting* to something as opposed to *responding* to it. To react is an instinctive action without meditation or thought before it occurs. But to respond, by contrast, means a thoughtful and calculated action based upon logical and deductive processes.

Based upon what Jesus spoke in Matthew's Gospel, *"Out of the fullness (the overflow, the superabundance) of the heart the mouth speaks."* (Matthew 12:34)

I think He was referring to what happens when we just *react* to a situation. A *reaction* will clearly show what is in the fullness, overflow and superabundance of your heart. If your heart is pure and in alignment with the will of Father God, it is probably okay to *react* to things. However, if you are (like most of us) still struggling with your flesh and its attempt to "take over," ~ fighting your thoughts for freedom in your inner self, and seeking selfish healing for your inner illnesses ~ it would be to your advantage to ask God to show you exactly how you should *respond* rather than *react* in various situations.

185

Responding to situations allows you the opportunity to rightfully take responsibility for your actions. *Reaction,* on the other hand usually results in blindly reacting with blame toward others or offering excuses (rationalizing) as to why you did (or didn't do) what was right.

For example, when someone at work criticizes your effort and attitude in a special project on which you are working, do you lash out with phrases similar to this? "Who are you to criticize me? I've seen some of your work and it is much worse than mine is; besides this is the best I can do since I have been so busy and stressed out lately." Does this a sound like a response or a reaction?

It is easy to observe the difference in someone else, but more difficult when it applies to yourself. Of course the above example is a *reaction.* It is filled with anger toward the one criticizing and overflows with horizontal comparison between the two of you. It contains the hint of an excuse because of stress and being busy.

A *response* would have occurred after examining if there was any truth in the criticism (refer to "How to handle and respond to criticism" in Chapter 5). You would then proceed to deal only with the truth that the criticism contains. This is *responding* rather than merely *reacting.* You might even find gratitude toward a person for pointing out needed areas of improvement.

Becoming "storm-proof" will not occur in your life unless you release and put to death the bitter attitudes kept alive by an unwillingness to forgive, from the heart, those persons, circumstances and situations that are causing the bitterness.

By *not* choosing to <u>respond</u> instead of <u>reacting</u> in situations of confrontation, criticism and censure, you open the door for rejection and resentment. This will also open the way into inner wounding that tends to cripple a believer's walk.

Why did Jesus not need inner healing? Have you ever thought about it?

Considering what happened to Jesus, you could conclude He needed inner healing more than anyone did. He was probably identified as an illegitimate child, since Mary was pregnant with Him before she married. His earthly father probably died while he was a teenager. Even his closest friends and disciples misunderstood him. He was mocked, jeered, ridiculed and rejected by the very people He came to save. The religious leadership finally sentenced him to die for blasphemy. He was killed in the most cruel and degrading manner by being hanged naked on a Roman cross.

Probably no one in history has been hurt more than Jesus, the Christ. I say this because He knew the hearts and minds of men. This knowledge and insight of men's hearts provided Him more understanding than any other human could ever know of the anger, rejection and hatred people bore toward Him. He would seem to be a candidate for inner healing if anyone ever was.

Instead, Jesus, was the healthiest man Who ever lived ~ physically, mentally and emotionally. Why? The reason Jesus never needed inner healing is that Jesus never *reacted* sinfully to what was said or done to Him. This statement contains the key to all inner healing.

For you, that means your health, wholeness, freedom from hurts ~ as seen from the perspective of eternity ~ has nothing to do with *how* you have been hurt. It has to do, instead, with the *way* you have *reacted* to that hurt.

Whatever has happened to you in the past (serious though it may be), you can be healed from its initial and continuing effects by your choices.

It is important for you to choose now to turn from sinful *reactions* and make righteous *responses.* When this occurs, you indeed are taking responsibility for your inner healing and moving towards becoming truly "storm free" from the soul storms facing you.

CHAPTER FIFTEEN

WALKING IN VICTORY

PRAYER OF SOLUTIONS

Abba, I ask for the blessings of Your Presence, provision, peace, purpose, plan, protection and promise, out of which comes my perspective and perseverance!

As you walk into and through the problems encountered in this journey called life, learning and employing the Lord's methods of facing, withstanding and overcoming the "blue northers" is most critical.

Listed in the above prayer are a variety of solutions available for the problems we face. Let's call it the "Prayer of Solutions." The first and most important is the blessing of the *Presence of the Lord.*

God's Presence

While in the *Presence of Jesus* there is no foe, no situation or circumstance that is too formidable for you to overcome or endure. As creator of all things, The Lord Jesus Christ knows everything that you are facing. He knows the dimension, duration and power of everything created. If you have invited Him to dwell within your heart and become your Lord, then He lives within you and you live within Him. The battles you face will then become His battles and victory is assured.

There are at least two types of the Lord's Presence. There is His <u>omnipresence</u> ~ the ever-present Person of the Lord in *all* places at *all* times. The word "Presence" as it is used in the above prayer does not refer to *this* particular appearance of God. What it does mean is the <u>manifest Presence</u> of God. This is the supernatural "showing up" (*or manifestation*) of God in a specific time and place so that His Presence can be sensed by humans. When God's <u>manifest Presence</u> appears, wondrous things occur. This is the Presence for which you should pray.

What your part of the equation is for enjoying this type Presence is to learn to die to self-so Jesus and His *manifest Presence* can live in your stead. The problem with dying to self is that it must be exercised continuously. Self wants to become resurrected and live independently from God's Presence and control.

The Presence of God demands worship as the only appropriate and proper response. This is evidenced by the scripture, "*That in (at) the name of Jesus every knee should (must) bow, in heaven and on earth, and every tongue [frankly and openly] confess and acknowledge that Jesus Christ is Lord, to the glory of God the Father.*" (Philippians 2:10-11)

Of course this is referring to the final reign when Jesus is crowned King of all the earth. However, it also applies to believers in the present. When you come into His Presence you only have the option to worship.

God is so pure, holy and righteous that responses and reactions of all created beings in His *manifest Presence* can only be those of worship. Man, by the design of his Creator, has a capacity and a hunger to worship. There is no other choice ~ if you don't worship God you will find a very unworthy substitute.

Worship (as has just been described) is the initial basis for conquering all the storms you face. That is why you need the *manifest Presence* of God in your life constantly.

God's Provision

The next item mentioned in the prayer is God's *provision*. Provision is a word meaning several things. Its primary meaning is an act of supplying or equipping. This alone is of sufficient value to be included in a list of things for which you should ask and depend upon God.

However, not only do you need God to supply and equip you, there is another facet of provision you need. It is that of preparation or having something in readiness. A stockpile (if you will) of necessary supplies available for your use when needed.

There are at least two reasons why you should ask God for His *provision* rather than what *you* want provided. One reason is the fact you don't know all the ingredients of your 'real needs.' Many things you think you need are really things that are not best or efficient for your development into a disciple of Christ. God's timing is perfect and oftentimes you do not know exactly "what" you need. Neither do you know the "when" of that need. God knows both and His provision is best.

Secondly, there are many things you have not realized you need that God will abundantly supply. Possibly you need a relationship with a particular personality type person who will prod you into a better walk in the ways of God ~ perhaps a person you would not choose to have in your life right now. This person can be a tool in the hand of God whom He will use to chip off the rough edges of your life, and help you become conformed to the image of Jesus.

The Sculptor's Skill or "How can I become Like Jesus?"

Once there was a little boy who went to school along the same route day after day. His path took him beside the studio of a great sculptor who was beginning to work on a large project. It was a huge granite rock easily observed by the little lad as he strolled by. Day after day the little boy watched as the huge granite bolder slowly changed into the figure of a horse.

The magnificent animal's nostrils were flared as the full flowing mane spewed backwards as if pulled by a resistant wind. The muscles of the legs were in splendid detail and showed the strain of the speed at which the granite sculpture galloped. The boy's most favorite animal in the whole wide world was a horse.

After several months had passed and the piece was almost finished, the little boy had occasion to meet and talk with the great sculptor. He was excited and anxious to find out the secret of the great man's success. He asked the question, "Sir, How did you get that great huge rock to look like this wonderful horse?"

The great sculptor was very wise and told the lad, "Son, I just took the tools I have, and chipped, chiseled, hammered and sanded away everything in that big old rock that didn't look like a horse."

This is the same way it is when *you* come to Jesus. You give Him the big misshapen mass of unfinished rock that you are now. And God takes His *provision* ~ the tools (persons and circumstances) He has made available ~ and chips, chisels, hammers and sands away everything in that big old ugly rock (you) that doesn't look like Christ until the image of Jesus is formed in you. The process is not pleasant or comfortable, but it is effective; and the final result is worth all the effort and sacrifice.

God's Peace

The next item in the "Prayer of Solutions" is God's *peace*. There is a definition of peace that is used in the Amplified translation of the Bible, (which I prefer). It is *"Freedom from all the distresses that are experienced as the result of sin."*

Can you imagine what it would be like to have a life that is free from the distresses of sin? The distresses of guilt and condemnation are gone. According to Jesus, when you accept Him and make Him Lord of your life in faith, you can expect to receive and walk in that kind of peace.

Most believers in Jesus are not aware that this kind of peace is part of the package of salvation. Unfortunately, we do not walk in the fullness of it most of the time. We are prone to agree with the state of affairs in life that surround us and walk out the bondage of our circumstances.

Peace is not the absence of conflict. It is the absence of *distress* during conflict.

When you ask for and receive the peace of God, you find you no longer have to walk in the bondage of your circumstances, but begin to walk in victory with Jesus.

"Peace I leave with you: My [own] peace I now give and bequeath to you. Not as the world gives do I give to you. Do not let your hearts be troubled, neither let them be afraid." (John 14:27)

Remember "My hope is built on nothing less than Jesus' blood and righteousness." Hope will precede faith and faith (in Jesus) gives me His *peace*.

God's Purpose

Purpose is described as the object toward which one strives or for which something exists. The object (for you) toward which God the Father strives, is for you to become conformed to the image of Christ. The object or *purpose* for which you exist is to worship and glorify God. This simplifies your life once you understand it. You are to become Christ-like and worship and glorify Abba. In this state you are completed, fulfilled and satisfied.

Consider what it is in your life that is not agreeing with the image of Jesus Christ and does not allow you to worship and glorify God as you are designed to. Abba could 'zap' you, and you would instantly be like Jesus; but He doesn't work that way. When you were conceived, God placed within your genetic make-up everything necessary for you to become like Jesus Christ. He also placed within you a 'free-will' so you could choose ~

choose to fall in love with Him, and let Him do the mighty work of conforming you in the image of Jesus, or choose to reject Him.

Satan, self and God has been in competition for your will and your choices. Each one wants you to choose his way. God's way and purpose is the only beneficial choice for your well being. The other choices result in your destruction. This is why you must make a conscious choice to yield your will to Abba for His *purpose* in your life.

God's Plan

God's *plan* for your life differs from His purpose. *Plan*, by definition, means a detailed scheme, program or method worked out *beforehand* for the accomplishment of an objective.

If God's purpose for you is to become conformed to the image of Christ, His *plan* for you is the *way* He will accomplish it.

There is an *easy way* and a *hard way* for this to be implemented. The *easy way* is choosing as early and as often as possible to yield your will to God's way of doing things. This sounds so amazingly simple; but both the flesh and its desires, and Satan and his desires for you, provide plenty of opportunities for detours.

The *hard way* of implementing God's plan is for you to stray from the accepted ways of life outlined in God's Word, experiment with the world and its flesh-pleasing ways, and/or seek the devil's counterfeits for all God has proposed.

God's grace and His mercy will always be available this side of death; but oh, the struggles and pains, failures and disappointments that accompany the *hard way*.

God includes (allows) these adversities in His plan of placing the necessary items in your life, so that when you are faced with desperate situations, your choices will lead to Him.

Early or late in your walk as a believer in Jesus Christ, you must choose to submit your will to the loving hands of Abba, Who will then begin to implement His individual *plan* for you.

God's Protection

In the Solution's Prayer, God's *protection* for you begins with choosing to put your trust in Him and His ways, and by not relying on your own thoughts, ideas or deductions for your safety. This is not bypassing your common sense, but is to remind you to rely on God. Testing God in areas you have not received permission to enter is not a good practice.

You can pray for God's *protection* over yourself or a loved one while travelling, at work, home or school, etc. and trust God to accomplish it. You are to work in concert with God in the problems you face. Remember though, He is the conductor and you are but a player in the orchestra. You must follow Him.

After asking God to help you, keep your spiritual ears open to hear any instructions He may want to give concerning how you might be getting into danger and how to avoid disaster.

God's Promise

God's *promise* to you is that He will never leave you or forsake you. *"I will not in any way fail you nor give you up nor leave you without support. [I will] not, [I will] not, [I will] not in any degree leave you helpless nor forsake nor let [you] down (relax My hold on you)! [Assuredly not!]"* (Hebrews 13:5b)

By definition, a *promise* is an assurance or declaration that one will or will not do a certain thing. There are many other *promises* of God to you, but perhaps the most important one is the one listed above. Remember those delays from God are not an indication of being forsaken. Someone said once, *"God is never late, but He sure has missed a lot of opportunities to be early!"*

I want to pray for the manifestation of God's promises for me.

Another important thing is the expected results: your *perspective* and your *perseverance*.

"And whatever you ask for in prayer, having faith and [really] believing, you will receive." (Matthew 21:22)

My Perspective

When you have received God's *Presence, Provision, Peace, Purpose, Plan, Protection and His Promise*, your *perspective* changes and your *persistence* is established.

A loose but apt definition of *perspective* is 'point of view.' With God's interaction, your point of view changes considerably. You begin to see things as He does, instead of strictly from your own (or that of the world's) viewpoint. This in turn causes you to develop and mature in all the fruit of the spirit available to you, including patience and self-control.

My Perseverance

The definition of *perseverance* is to persist in, or remain constant to, a purpose, idea or task, in the face of discouragement or opposition.

When applied spiritually, you can see the need of *perseverance* as you face the assignments God has for you. More believers fail in their walk toward maturity because of a lack of *perseverance* than any other factor. Obstacles and opposition arise and send you into a tailspin of depression and despondency.

Part of the process God has for His children is to learn the lesson of 'stick-with-it' in spite of conflict and hostility. The reader is urged to repeat the following prayer often.

PRAYER OF SOLUTIONS

Abba, I ask for the blessings of Your Presence, provision, peace, purpose, plan, protection and promise, out of which comes my *perspective* and *perseverance*!

It is my belief that by using this prayer regularly, God will grant you an effective walk of victory over the 'blue northers.'

Through the Great "I AM" — I am — ?

If I were to ask you to name ten things about yourself that you do not like or are negative traits, you would have little trouble listing them. Instead, I am asking for five positive traits you would like to be known by. I want you to be very specific rather than vague or too broad in your descriptions.

One way of approaching this is to think what you would like to have inscribed on your tombstone as an epitaph. These may be traits not yet achieved, but what you would desire to have said about you.

Remember that man (you) is made in the image of God. When God speaks a thing, what He says happens. Therefore, you can also speak things that have the potential of becoming a self-fulfilling prophecy. (*This is another reason you must watch what comes out of your mouth whether good or evil.*)

I have listed below the positive traits by which I would like to be known. You are welcome to use them as you own or list others. The prayer is a simple one, but it is also most profound.

Abba, in obedience to Your Word, I speak this:
Through the Great I AM, I am: loving, anointed, confident, courageous, efficient, holy, submitted and wise.

Now I would like to explain why I chose these traits.

Loving. I want to be known as *loving* because God is the essence of love. He is not just about love, He is love itself. The biggest difference in the way of the world and the way of God is love. *"But God shows and clearly proves His [own] love for us by the fact that while we were still sinners, Christ (the Messiah, the Anointed One) died for us."* (Romans 5:8)

"For God so greatly loved and dearly prized the world that He [even] gave up His only begotten (unique) Son, so that whoever believes in (trusts in, clings to, relies on) Him shall not perish (come to destruction, be lost) but have eternal (everlasting) life." (John 3:16)

Anointed. To be *anointed* by God is another trait by which I wish to be known. Without His anointing, I can have no power to live the life to which God calls me or fulfill the assignments He has given me. Anointing is a gift from God and follows a call from God. Anointing carries with it the power to accomplish what the call encompasses. To attempt to carry out an assignment without the anointing is to digress into human ability alone (a disaster).

We must be very careful not to try to duplicate what God has done in someone else's life under a different anointing, or in your own life in times past. God's anointing, like His mercy, is new and fresh every morning.

As mentioned earlier, the word "Christ" is a Greek word for The Anointed One. "Messiah" is the Hebrew word for the same Person, The Anointed One. When Christ lives in me, I have His anointing *within* me. When I am given an assignment (a call if you will) God's anointing rests *upon* me. I am in need of anointing both *within* and *upon* me in order to walk in power under God's direction.

Confident. The next trait in my list of epitaphs is that of being *confident.* Many of us (myself included) have self-confidence problems. I want to substitute *God-confidence* for the word *self-confidence.* I then have no need to rely on myself, but instead put my complete confidence in God and His ability to accomplish what He wants in my life. My only response is that of obedience to what His instructions are.

Confidence in God accompanies faith and allows me to embrace trust and reliance on the Father, knowing I will see the desired results (His desires not mine). A by-product of confidence is *boldness.* I no longer have to function under fear and timidity, for now I have boldness because I am *confident.*

Courageous. The reason I want to be *courageous* is that I need courage to face things I do not want to face. There are many things I *know* to do, but I lack *courage* to do them. *Courage* is defined as the quality or state of mind or spirit, enabling one to face danger or hardship with confidence and resolution ~ to be brave. Many times I have turned another way rather than face a danger or hardship. I need the *courage* of God in my life.

Efficient. To be *efficient* is to employ the wise use of my time, treasure and talent. My time is used with focus on complete efficiency in time management (work, play, rest and refreshing). My treasure is utilized in planting its seed into the Kingdom of God and seeing the thirty, sixty and hundred fold returns (having my needs met and having a surplus to share with others). My talents are to be employed to bring honor to, and glorify God.

Efficiency is not the organization of time, treasure and talents so that every second and resource is used. It is instead the use of all my life so that when I leave this world, I shall not regret any effort to which I have put my hand. That is to be truly *efficient*.

Holy. One of the latter traits listed is that of being *holy*. Noah Webster writes in his American Dictionary of the English Language concerning the word holy: properly, whole, entire or perfect, in a moral sense. Hence, holy means pure in heart, temper or dispositions; free from sin and sinful affections.

Man, by receiving Christ, can indeed become holy in his intentions, motivations and thoughtlife. Immediately upon being convicted of sin, confess, repent and accept the forgiveness offered by Jesus' sacrifice, thereby becoming holy. *"But as the One Who called you is holy, you yourselves also be holy in all your conduct and manner of living. For it is written, You shall be holy, for I am holy."* (1 Peter 1:15-16)

Submitted. This word has been bandied about with various meanings for years, many of them very wrong to say the least.

One of the most misused and confused definitions applies to our women and the way in which they are supposed to submit as wives to their husbands.

The usual use of this definition by most husbands is something like this. "The Bible says, wives submit to (obey) your husbands therefore you do as I say." Let's look at two words which, with proper application, will help shed some light in understanding the correct meaning.

The first word is *authority*. By definition, authority is the right and power to command, enforce laws, exact obedience, determine or judge. It also means freedom or right granted to another (authorization). Authority is also defined as an accepted source of expert information or advice. Another facet of the meaning of authority is power to influence or persuade resulting from knowledge or experience.

The second word mentioned is the word *submit*. Its meaning is also varied and begins with, to surrender or yield oneself to the will or authority of another. Submit is also defined as to being subject to a condition or process. It is further defined as the committing of something to the consideration or judgement of another.

The best definition I believe is this, *to submit to someone is to allow that one to be who or what he or she is called or positioned by God to be.*

To be submitted in the sense of its use in Paul's writings to the Corinthians directed to wives, is to be yielded to the authority of God first of all and permanently. By this I mean that God's delegation of authority is from Himself to the husband, then to the wife, then to the children. However, every believer's primary submission of authority is to God first, then to the ranking of earthly power God has established. In any conflict with authorities, I must always yield to the *highest* authority. This is what I would call an *attitude* of submission.

When Peter and John were called before the religious rulers of their day and told not to teach anymore in the Name of Jesus they replied, *"Whether it is right in the sight of God to listen to you and obey you rather than God, you must decide (judge). But we ourselves cannot help telling what we have seen and heard."* (Acts 4:19-20) *"Then Peter and the apostles replied, We must obey God rather than men."* (Acts 5:29)

They were in an *attitude* of submission and were compelled from within to obey the *highest* authority. So it must be for us all. We are to attempt to submit to our earthly authority as much as possible. We allow them to become all that they are called and positioned to be, i.e. submitting to a husband is to allow him to be everything God has called or positioned him to be as a husband. To submit to a wife is to allow her to be all she has been called and positioned by God to become as a wife. This can be done with an attitude of submission.

However, when that earthly authority commands an action contrary to the Word of God, we then submit to the higher authority. A woman does not have to obey, by *behavior,* every command of her husband but in her *attitude* of submission, she can still be true to her vows of marriage.

Before Paul wrote the submission verses to wives, husbands, children, etc. he wrote this verse: *"Be subject to one another out of reverence for Christ (the Messiah, the Anointed One)."* (Ephesians 5:21)

Wise. The last trait I have listed as an epitaph is that of being *wise.*

Perhaps the reader is familiar with the term meekness and its equestrian meaning. When a horse is saddle broken its energy and strength are not compromised. The horse is brought under the control of a rider who communicates through clicking sounds of the tongue, the use of a bridle and bit, also by pressure of the rider's knees and heels, as well as other methods. There is also a measure of trust developed between the horse and rider, this is known as *meekness* or 'power under control.'

In no way does meekness imply weakness, merely that the great power of the horse is 'under control.' So it must be with man. God spoke of Moses, " *Now the man Moses was very meek (gentle, kind and humble) or above all the men on the face of the earth.*" (Numbers 12:3) He also gives a promise to the meek in Matthew's Gospel, *"Blessed are the meek for they shall inherit the earth."* (Matthew 5:5)

I said all that in order to say these things. Since meekness means power under control, in the same way I think *wisdom is knowledge and facts ' under control.'*

Knowledge is of the head; but wisdom is of the heart.

You and I are bombarded daily with a myriad of data. These include statistics, facts and information, both in the natural and spiritual realms (scientific, economic, business, relationships, Biblical facts and revelation, etc.). As long as they remain informational data without application they are of no more use than a database or a set of encyclopedia.

Vast amounts of information are available, but as long as they remain informational data without application, they are of no more use than a database or a set of encyclopedia. I want to be able to take this available data and, through wise choices, live as God wants me to live, using His wisdom in all phases of my everyday life.

Therefore, to be *wise* is to correctly use knowledge, facts and information at my disposal in all my decisions. I want to be known as a man who is *wise*.

To the believer who is interested in solving the soul storms in life, the answers in this prayer will be of much aid in doing so.

Abba, in obedience to Your Word, I speak this:
Through the Great I AM, I am: loving, anointed, confident, courageous, efficient, holy, submitted and wise.

CONCLUSION

The word conclusion has several meanings. *To bring to an end or close* is the most prevalent. I find myself struggling with the fact that I cannot bring this message to an end, I can only close. In fact, this book is but a genesis (a beginning), not an end. It offers only a glimpse into the understanding of how to withstand the soul storms in our lives.

This will agree with still another definition of the word conclusion, which is *the outcome or result of an act or process*. The term 'process' has been mentioned many times over the course of these pages, and a process is the way God prepares His children to rule and reign with Him while on this earth. This process will probably never be an instantaneous occurrence, because the basic nature of a believer needs time to change and become like Jesus.

A process must have the desired *result* or *outcome* from God's perspective for it to be successful. This includes learning where attacks come from and what God wants to train us to do about them. In human beings this takes time, both the time of *Chronos* (the passing of time as in the ticking of a clock) and *Kairos* (time passing in a season such as maturation or growth).

It has been said that a believer's maturity is best identified by the way in which he handles adversity. God allows storms for us to practice and develop correct ways to deal with adversity.

Paul exhorts believers to imitate his example when we face adversity. *"The things you have learned and received and heard and seen in me, practice these things; and the God of peace shall be with you.* " (Philippians 4:9)

The book of Proverbs sheds God's light on many wonderful topics. The subject of soul storms in our life is no exception. *"Be not afraid of sudden terror and panic, nor he stormy blast or the storm and ruin of the wicked when it comes [for you will be guiltless], For the Lord shall be your confidence, firm and strong, and shall keep your foot from being caught [in a trap] or some hidden danger. Withhold not good from those to whom it is due [its rightful owners], when it is in your hand to do it.* " (Proverbs 3:25-27)

There is a very important word contained in the first sentence of the above passage. It is the word *when*. There is no doubt that storms *will* be coming into a believer's life the only question is *when* will they occur. Since we have the guarantee of the storms, we need to truly learn how to become "storm proof."

I have used that term (storm proof) through out this reading. It is my wish that you are first of all aware that there will be times and places of distress and discomfort in your life.

Secondly, I wish you to know that God has provided for you, through His grace, methods of remedy for these storms.

Lastly, I wish you to become a warrior in God's army to join our Lord Jesus, the Christ, in destroying the works of the devil.

As you read (and I hope re-read) the various methods used by the devil and our flesh to steal, kill and destroy, you will recognize and use these methods more readily. Hopefully, when these attacks occur your spiritual senses will have been sharpened, the spiritual weapons will have been made ready, and you will be able to withstand the soul storms of adversity so as to rule and reign over the circumstances of life.

This marvelous journey our Lord has orchestrated for each one of us is 'custom made' to bring out our best. It will use our strengths and cause our weaknesses to be made strong in Him. It will eliminate sin by ending evil thought patterns. The process will change wicked patterns of behavior and susceptibility to failure into the magnificent image of Jesus Christ within each of us.

If nothing else is known about these soul storms but what I have written, it will be enough to stop the inward warring for supremacy between our soul and spirit. We will gladly yield to the Holy Spirit's message uttered through our spirit man and accept what God is doing and is going to do in our lives.

Still another meaning of 'conclusion' that is most intriguing to me: *a decision reached after deliberation.* It is my hope and desire that the reader deliberates or thinks seriously about the message of this book, then makes a quality decision concerning that deliberation.

Or still another way to put it is, make a quality decision to listen and wait on God's Word (His voice) in all areas of life *before* making any other decisions.

Throughout this book I have also been attempting to share with you the gifts and experiences God has revealed to my wife and me. It is my ardent desire and petition before the Father, that this information will be yet another method through which He chooses to reveal His nature and mysteries to you, the reader.

It is through the revelation of God in each heart that each of us can become "storm proof" to withstand the 'blue northers' of soul storms life brings our way.

"He who has ears [to hear], let him be listening and let him consider and perceive and comprehend by hearing." (Matthew 13:9)

— Selah —

FOR ADDITIONAL COPIES OF THIS BOOK

SOLVING

SOUL

STORMS

Become **STORM-PROOF** rather than **STORM-FREE!**

by

Using God's remedies for man's problems!

A new book for today's problems by

NORMAN R. HEMPHILL

Prices

Single Copies of SSS:	**$16** (includes $4 shipping)
Two copies of SSS:	**$30** (includes $4 shipping)
Three copies of SSS:	**$45** (includes $4 shipping)
Five copies of SSS:	**$65** (includes $6 shipping)

Call 1-817-514-0653 for credit card orders or mail check to:
All Nations Publications, P.O. Box 92847, Southlake, Texas 76092

Is healing and miracle ministry generally unreliable, unpredictable and sometimes mysterious to you? What prevents you from healing the sick and performing miracles like the Savior and His disciples? The author of this book reveals how his ministry of healing became much more effective, predictable and reliable as the Holy Spirit adjusted him with the scriptural truths that he reveals in this book. As the author has preached these truths in his traveling ministry, thousands have been healed as hundreds of believers have experienced the power of God working their first healing or miracle through them. More mature believers at these meetings have often  developed a greater consistency in helping the suffering. No doubt that the readers of this book will be refreshed, adjusted, and strengthened in faith. They will be more able to help many more suffering people and duplicate the Savior's ministry.

"The 1990's is a decade characterized by the rise of the modern day apostolic movement. *The Last Apostles on Earth* is, therefore, very timely. It provides us with valuable biblical information for building a theological framework within to understand this work of the Holy Spirit in our day." *Dr. C. Peter Wagner, Fuller Seminary*

"*The Last Apostles on Earth* is a fresh and unique look at what Scripture says about apostolic ministry. This book is a must read for anyone wanting to account for the biblical evidence regarding apostles in the Church today." *Dr. Gary Greig, Professor, Regent Univ. School of Theology*

Ministries Today Magazine Review: "If you thought the latest wave of revival manifestations stirred up the church, wait until the next one crests! The author of this new book says that the next big revival wave will bring genuine apostolic ministry to the surface. Dr. Roger Sapp believes that in the latter part of the 1990's, Christ will freshly call, restore and anoint apostles as gift ministries to the church. This author writes in order to prepare local leaders to relate to these mobile ministers, and he explores and applies biblical principles about apostles. Roger Sapp, (formerly) a theology teacher at a Virginia college, explores Old Testament kings as types of New Testament apostles. That analogy, though limited, helps show how apostles conduct the affairs of the Kingdom of God. Many insights await any careful reader... This book does not simply study apostles as a topic. Apostles come alive as real people sent from God and as the Lord's final thrust to bring the Church age to a glorious close. If the church is to obey the Great Commission before Jesus returns, the author contends, we will need to end with even greater power than the first apostles displayed. As end-time revival waves break upon humanity, this book urges us to grab our surfboards and prepare for the last great ride of church history: the whole church reaching the whole world with the whole gospel. "

"I really appreciate Roger Sapp's approach to this important subject. He seeks to arrive at a biblical answer in the face of an emotionally charged environment. You may not agree, but you'll face some real questions head on". Dudley Hall, President, Successful Christian Living Ministries

What does the Bible teach concerning women in ministry? Is there a difference between men and women in roles in the Church? Is "equality" in the Church taught by the Bible? Is there a biblical reason to make exceptions for the normal "rules" for certain women?

Pandora's Pulpit answers these questions and many others candidly and courageously. It exposes the extremes presently being taught and practiced in the Church. *Pandora's Pulpit* is destined to become a classic on the role of women in the present renewal.

Pandora's Pulpit offers a summary of various modern attempts to reject the New Testament's basic teaching concerning women and their role in the Church. It reveals the divine reasons why the New Testament teaches what it does about women's ministries. Most importantly this book describes the predictable outcomes of teaching disobedience to these important New Testament truths in the lives of women, men and their children.

Also Available from the Publisher:
Apostolic Fathers and Spiritual Bastards
A Biblical Review of the Essential Ministry Father Doctrine
1999, 110 pages, $7.00
Order from All Nations Publications 1-817-514-0653

Controversial title? Let us explain. In early 1998, Roger Sapp heard messages from prominent leaders and read four recent and popular charismatic books that were teaching a unkind and false doctrine about modern apostles and discipling others. As a result, he has written a courageous and pointed book that addresses the following questions: What does the Bible teach concerning modern apostolic fathers and their relationships with other Christians? Do these ministry

fathers save spiritual sons from being spiritual bastards? Is an intimate relationship with a ministry father essential to please God? Are ministries inherited from ministry fathers? Do all properly prepared ministries become ministry fathers? Is the true foundation of spiritual inheritance in the Kingdom of God the relationships between fathers and sons? What does the apostle Paul's phrase *you have not many fathers* really mean? In this new book, Roger Sapp answers these questions and many others as he confronts this very popular heresy head on. He compares with Scripture and with insight analyzes this unkind and unscriptural teaching that unfairly marks some Christians as *spiritual bastards* or orphans. He calls the Church back to a balanced and scriptural approach to apostolic ministry and the discipleship of others. Every leader needs to read this courageous and pointed book! This book is subtitled *A Biblical Review of the Essential Ministry Father Doctrine.* It is 110 pages and includes the popular *Honoring the Truth-teller* articles as an appendix.